Coming Together for the Sake of God

Contributions to Jewish-Christian Dialogue from Post-Holocaust Germany

Edited by
Hanspeter Heinz
and
Michael A. Signer

A Michael Glazier Book

LITURGICAL PRESS
Collegeville, Minnesota

www.litpress.org

A Michael Glazier Book published by Liturgical Press.

Originally published in German: Hanspeter Heinz (Hg.). *Um Gottes willen miteinander verbunden. Der Gespraechskreis "Juden und Christen" beim Zentralkomitee der deutschen Katholiken,* LIT Verlag, Münster 2004.

Cover design by Ann Blattner. Photo: Pier Paolo Cito/Pool/Corbis.

1 2 3 4 5 6 7 8

Library of Congress Catalog-in-Publication Data

Coming together for the sake of God : contributions to Jewish-Christian dialogue from post-Holocaust Germany / edited by Hanspeter Heinz and Rabbi Michael A. Signer.

p. cm.

"A Michael Glazier Book."

ISBN-13: 978-0-8146-5167-4 (alk. paper)

1. Judaism—Relations—Christianity. 2. Christianity—Relations—Judaism. 3. Jews—Germany—History—1945- 4. Jews—Germany—Intellectual life—20th century. I. Heinz, Hanspeter. II. Signer, Michael Alan.

BM535.C6165 2006

261.2'60943—dc22 2006017008

With Thanks

The editors want to acknowledge the support of Mr. Kurt Simon and the Kurt and Tessye Simon Fund for Jewish Studies at the University of Notre Dame in the publication of this volume. Mr. Simon left Germany for America during the rise of National Socialism and graduated from the University of Notre Dame. His generosity now enables Jews and Christians to learn about the remarkable steps by the Jewish-Christian Discussion Group of the Central Committee of German Catholics toward reconciliation in the lands where the *Shoah* began. May the words of the Discussion Group become a sign of hope.

Hanspeter Heinz
Michael A. Signer

Contents

Responses to the Work of the Discussion Group

Appendices

Preface

The discussion group "Jews and Christians" of the Central Committee of German Catholics was created in 1971. Nowhere else in the world did a country's highest committee of lay people found an organization for dialogue between Jews and Christians with the goal of fostering mutual relations. The discussion group is also unique in that, right from the start, it dared to enter into a theological conversation. Together, Christians and Jews in this group have published statements on fundamental questions and on current affairs, thus making a German contribution to a "theology after Auschwitz" that has been acclaimed internationally but is not well enough known outside of Germany, even among specialists.

Michael A. Signer, Professor of Jewish Thought and Culture at the University of Notre Dame, Indiana, and John T. Pawlikowski, O.S.M., Professor of Ethics at the Catholic Theological Union, Chicago, supported the Central Committee's initiative to publish the documents in English so that this theological voice from Germany might be heard in English language countries and internationally.

This volume contains an introduction to the discussion group's self-understanding and work as well as a collection of its publications. In addition, we asked several experts from the United States, two Jewish, two Catholic, and one Protestant from Germany, to write their own thoughts on the importance of the discussion group's declarations for Jewish-Christian dialogue. Thus, our invitation to conversation is extended in a dialogical way.

We are grateful to our American friends Michael A. Signer and John Pawlikowski for their advice in planning this book, for their having found a publisher, and for their statements. We also want to thank our publisher, the Liturgical Press. We owe particular thanks to Sr. Katherine Wolff, N.D.S., Jerusalem, who was responsible for the translation as a whole, as well as to the other translators, Claus Jungkunz, Martha Matesich, Thomas Norris, Elisabeth Petuchowski, Helga Sourek, and Colleen Wunsch. Finally, I thank my secretary, Ms. Irmgard Hemprich, and my colleagues, Professor Herbert Immenkoetter and Dr. Johann Ev. Hafner, assistant professor in our department, who have given their support to the project at every stage along the way. Finally, we express our profound thanks to Molly Zahn and Emily Hartzer of the University of Notre Dame who assisted in the preparation of this volume.

Augsburg, July 2006
Hanspeter Heinz
Michael A. Signer

Foreword

The twentieth century witnessed the worst persecution to which the Jewish people has been subjected in its long history, a persecution whose goal was their utter extinction. But the twentieth century also witnessed a profound historical change in the relationship between Jews and Christians. The Second Vatican Council's declaration *Nostra aetate* (1965) can be seen as a milestone and the definitive turning point in this relationship. The Catholic Church regretted and condemned all forms of anti-Semitism and acknowledged its own Jewish roots. Since then, and in spite of various difficulties, dialogue and collaboration between the two faith communities has made considerable progress all over the world.

Pope John Paul II had an important role in fostering this dialogue and gave it important impulses. Let us remember above all his meeting with representatives of the Jewish community in Mainz during his first visit to Germany (1980), his visit to the Great Synagogue in Rome (1986), where the Pope spoke of the Jews as our elder brothers in the faith of Abraham, the establishment of diplomatic relations between Israel and the Holy See (1993), and his historic visit to Jerusalem during the Jubilee Year (2000).

Because of the tragic events in connection with the *Shoah,* Jewish-Christian dialogue in Germany is of particular importance and German Christians bear a special responsibility for post-Holocaust discussion. We are grateful to the discussion group "Jews and Christians," which has existed since 1971 as part of the Central Committee of German Catholics, for having taken up this dialogue at a high level and made some valuable contributions. In doing so, it connected with an important earlier tradition marked by such names as Leo Baeck, Franz Rosenzweig, and Martin Buber, and it could use the *Freiburger Rundbrief,* founded in 1948 by Gertrud Luckner, as a point of reference. We welcome the publication of these contributions in a collection that will be accessible to a broader international public.

Alongside the ecumenical dialogue between the Christian churches and the interfaith dialogue with the non-Christian religions, the dialogue between Jews and Christians has its own special character. Jews and Christians are linked in a unique relationship that does not exist between other religions. It is this closeness and at the same time the fundamental difference that makes this dialogue both difficult and full of promise, because Jews and Christians can bring a great common religious and humane heritage to the present and future problems of humanity. Thus Jewish-Christian dialogue is one of the signs of hope in our time.

Rome, July 2006
Walter Cardinal Kasper
President,
Pontifical Commission for Religious Relations with Judaism

Foreword

The terrible persecution of the Jewish people under the twentieth-century regime of National Socialism still weighs heavily on Germany. In this regard, declarations of guilt are not enough. We may ask for forgiveness, but we may not forget. Nor may we overlook the underlying anti-Jewish attitudes that were dominant in Europe in antiquity, even before Christianity began, as well as in Christianity's institutional churches, which, in spite of some reductions in the violence, helped to prepare the atrocities.

After 1945 a new way of thinking developed in many areas, thanks be to God. Numerous documents from various countries testify to an intense willingness to enter into dialogue between Christians and Jews. The main churches in our country intensified their confrontation with and examination of the terrible events, insofar as that is at all possible. For Catholics, the discussion group "Jews and Christians," which has existed since 1971 as part of the Central Committee of German Catholics, plays an eminent part in this. The German Bishops' Conference has always had reconciliation with the Jewish people in mind, as can be seen in a number of documents, but they considered this matter to be in good hands with the above mentioned discussion group and with other initiatives such as the *"Freiburger Rundbrief,"* and in scholarly theological discussion. Thus, although there is a working team within the German Bishops' Conference, there is no commission for relations with the Jews. As for the discussion group, it is also important that its participants are both Jews and Christians and that together they bear responsibility for all publications.

The discussion group has not only understood the important steps taken after the Second Vatican Council and supported in particular the statements made in the declaration *Nostra aetate.* Along the lines of the Council, it has done valuable foundational work as well in this new epoch of dialogue. But it has also had the courage to discuss delicate topics, and to publish its insights. This includes reflection on the *Shoah* in the context of the declaration of the Vatican Commission for Religious Relations with the Jews of March 16, 1998. Let us not forget the discussion on "Convent and Cross in Auschwitz?" The new *Catechism of the Catholic Church* gave rise to a reaction regarding the way it discussed Jews and Judaism. Finally, the group did not shy away from the question of how to speak of guilt, suffering, and reconciliation fifty years after the *Reichskristallnacht* (Night of Broken Glass) of 1938, without simply repeating old statements, though those are certainly not wrong. But they not only looked at critical topics, which include above all one's way of dealing with Auschwitz. A brochure published in 1974, *A Journey to the Holy Land*, which was revised both in 1984 and in 1998, gave much valuable information and advice.

One characteristic of this dialogue is the way in which it has been led and has published on the various individual topics. The discussion group not only worked together with Jewish experts when writing its statements; Jewish voices and reactions were often gathered from other countries, particularly from the United States of America, after the writing was completed and during the public presentation of statements. Thus the conversation has been dialogical right in the way statements were written and presented. This not only gave it great credibility, but also inspired people in church and in society to study the texts. This was one reason, and not the least important one, why the texts were appreciated and welcomed in such a positive way.

I warmly welcome the fact that this experiment is now being presented again in a larger context by means of a special publication, and that again it is enlarged through fundamental statements by Jews and Christians. These shed a critical external light on the results and inspire further work on the central topics. The publication of both German and American editions is an important help in this. I thank not only the discussion group "Jews and Christians" in the Central Committee of German Catholics, but also those who initiated this publication; and I thank all who participated in the discussion of the individual texts and of the overall publication for their valuable collaboration. And above all, I hope that the book will be received everywhere in a friendly and fruitful way. For this I ask God's blessing.

Mainz, July 2003
Karl Cardinal Lehmann
President, German Bishops' Conference

Presentation of the Discussion Group "Jews and Christians"

Hanspeter Heinz

The discussion group "Jews and Christians," organized by the Central Committee of German Catholics *(Zentralkomitee der deutschen Katholiken = ZdK),* has been in existence for more than thirty years now. At present it has ten Jewish and sixteen Catholic members. Since 1979 it has authored several theological publications that are acknowledged internationally among experts and widely read in Germany.

Before describing the phases and results of our dialogue, I shall briefly introduce the Central Committee and its discussion group. Catholic lay organizations, with a total of five million members, have been working together on a national level within the Central Committee for 150 years. Their views on basic and current church and social responsibilities help to shape public opinion. The largest event is the Catholic Convention *(Katholikentag),* at which, every two years, about 100,000 people from all over the country, most of them young, get together for a week of worship, lectures, workshops, and meetings. Here, and at the parallel Protestant Convention *(Kirchentag),* thousands of Catholics and non-Catholics encounter Jews, their culture and history, for the first time in their lives. The very first workshop on "Communities and their Jewish Fellow Citizens" was in 1970 at the Catholic Convention in Trier, and it was from here that a proposal was sent to the *ZdK* to establish a permanent committee to be responsible for planning a Jewish-Christian contribution to every future Catholic congress.

Enthusiasm for a discussion group was kindled when, on behalf of the Central Committee, its ecclesiastical director, Professor Klaus Hemmerle, later Bishop of Aachen, put out feelers for Jewish participation in the first ecumenical Church Convention in Germany, the 1971 Pentecost meeting in Augsburg. When we (I had just been named assistant director) approached the Basel Professor Ernst Ludwig Ehrlich, a well-known Jewish scholar, with the idea, we were surprised to learn that he had come to Augsburg with the same purpose in mind. Thus, that same year, the Central Committee established the discussion group "Jews and Christians." In 1974 I was appointed chairman of the group. As its activities gathered momentum it was only natural that the group's original objective of contributing to the Catholic Convention, which they still actively do today, expanded, and the group gradually took on more responsibilities such as:

- presenting Jews and Judaism correctly in churches, schools, and universities, for example, by revising new editions of the Bible, materials for religious instruction, and history textbooks for schools;
- intensifying relations between the church and Jewish people, including trips to Israel, New York, Hungary, Poland, and Paris;
- organizing workshops and congresses for reflection on basic philosophical and theological issues; several publications have been translated into English, French, Polish, and Hungarian;
- preparing statements on current affairs on behalf of the President of the Central Committee, such as the Vatican recognition of the State of Israel or the pilgrimage of John Paul II to Jerusalem in 2000.

The discussion group organized by the Central Committee is a unique theological forum of Jews and Christians. Unlike other groups of its kind, which are actively involved in adult education and public relations in most German cities, it publishes theological statements. Although the study group for "Questions on Judaism" within the German Bishops' Conference writes theological and pastoral statements on Christian-Jewish relations, it has no Jewish experts. The theological faculties of state universities and church institutions of higher education are either Catholic, Protestant, or Jewish. Although Christian and Jewish communities often come together—after the recent arrival of 130,000 Jews from the former Soviet Union, about 100,000 Jews are now registered in Jewish communities in Germany[1]—there is no dialogue between them. The Central Council of Jews in Germany supports the Jewish population in matters of political, cultural, and other public concern, but does not become involved in religious issues. In contrast to all other initiatives, the discussion group organized by the Central Committee is neither a political lobby for Jewish interests nor a sponsor of educational events. As a national organ for theological dialogue, it is the only Jewish-Christian committee of its kind in Europe.

Without doubt, and despite a few setbacks, the Second Vatican Council's declaration *Nostra aetate,* § 4, marks an irreversible turning point in history. The Catholic Church officially brought to an end the almost two thousand years of estrangement and hostility towards Jews, and the resulting public declarations and meetings between Jews and Christians are encouraging. But equally important is the spiritual process experienced by individuals and discussion groups such as ours when, as required by the Council, they enter into a Christian-Jewish partnership. Basically, the work of our group can be divided into six stages.

1. Auschwitz: never again!

Initially it was our Jewish partners' desire to effectively overcome misunderstandings and ignorance about Judaism that determined their interest in a Jewish-Catholic relationship. It seemed that the threat of a "new Auschwitz" was still alive. Our first discussions often took the form of a theological examination of *Nostra aetate,* § 4. It was not that the members of our group were thought to be anti-Semitic. The "exam" referred far more to undesirable and inconspicuous forms of anti-Judaism. We were thus confronted with questions such as: In your opinion, were the Pharisees at the time of Jesus hypocrites? What do you think about the Jews being accused of murdering God? Do you consider the Old Testament to be out of date? Do you, as Christians, claim to have higher

1. A small number compared to the twenty-four million Catholics in Germany. The Russian Jews lived in a community that either rejected or punished religious conduct. For very different reasons they emigrated to either Israel, the United States, or Germany. For the most part those fearing anti-Semitism came to Germany, although they were not particularly interested in anything to do with Judaism, which resulted in limited dialogue on the Jewish side. Cf. Volker Resing, "Heimisch-Werden. Jüdisches Leben in Deutschland heute," *Herder Korrespondenz* 57 (2003) 172–77.

ethics, a better developed humanity, or beliefs superior to ours? What do you think about the distinction between the Jewish "God of justice" and the Christian "God of love"?

Although the Catholic members of our group had followed the radical changes brought about by the Council with interest and commitment, we had to admit that such questions often caused us embarrassment. We had only just begun to understand the consequences of *Nostra aetate.* During this wholesome learning process we Christians were struck by the fact that, to a large extent, we determined our identity, to the detriment of the Jews, by inwardly judging them to be theologically and ethically inferior. Because Jews disclosed the way they saw themselves to us, we Christians were obliged in many respects to amend our prejudicial understanding of Judaism, at the same time modifying the way we saw ourselves. The informative phase required careful rethinking.

In order to spread our insights into Judaism among Christians by means of conferences, conventions, and revised religious education and history, the discussion group at the University of Freiburg, led by the professor of religious education, Günter Biemer, and the professor of exegesis, Peter Fiedler, suggested that a research project be set up. The aim was to give Catholic teachers reliable guidelines for structuring their religious education classes. The result of this project is the four-volume handbook "The Learning Process of Christians and Jews" *(Lernprozess Christen-Juden).*

A further consequence of the need for authentic information about Judaism was a series of study tours to Israel for the executives of the Central Committee and members of the discussion group in 1975 and 1981. There we learned not only about the diversity and vitality of Judaism, but also about the enormous difficulties of establishing a Jewish culture and democracy in an autonomous state, after almost two thousand years of Diaspora, while remaining loyal to Jewish traditions and at the same time respecting the rights of non-Jewish citizens. One of the fruits of these trips was the booklet "A Journey to the Holy Land," its main intent being to show why this country is holy to Jews, Christians, and Muslims, each in their own way. Further trips followed, in 1986 to New York, the city with the largest Jewish Diaspora, and in 1991 to Hungary, where there are still about 100,000 Jews and where Christian-Jewish dialogue was just beginning. The trip to Poland in 1993 opened our eyes to the fact that reconciliation between Christians and Jews cannot succeed without German-Polish reconciliation. The most recent trip was in 1999 to Paris, the city with the largest Jewish population in Europe (600,000 Jews). A variety of lasting contacts was established during all these journeys.

2. Dialogue needs contemporary partnership

After we had worked together for several years there was no longer any doubt that our Catholic partners had also accepted the radical turning point in Christian-Jewish relations brought about by the Second Vatican Council. We Christians accepted the fact that if Christianity was to stay alive, it must remain rooted in the Judaism of the past and present. According to the apostle Paul (Rom 9–11), the root bears the tree and Israel bears the church. At the same time we wanted to know how important Christians and their faith are to Jews and their existence. Despite the asymmetry in the relationship, since Jews can be Jews without reference to Christians, an answer such as "Your faith has nothing to do with us!" would prevent true dialogue with reference to the present from ever really getting off the ground.

Reflecting on these issues caused embarrassment to both partners. We Catholics, for example, realized that we were treating the Jews with the same prejudices and reproaches directed at us by Protestants and against which we had been fighting since the Reformation and up to the beginning of ecumenical dialogue. During the period of apologetics Catholics were considered by Protestants to be a visible memorial of the unfortunate past, when Rome declared that good deeds and obedience to holy laws were more important than the Protestant doctrine of faith and divine mercy. In this view, Martin Luther and the other reformers had finally lifted Rome's restrictions, thus freeing all the children of God. Were we Catholics not putting the Jews down with the same outdated pattern of reasoning?

Our Jewish partners came to the conclusion that they, too, were preventing a truly contemporary dialogue so long as they were satisfied that their Jewish identity could be fully developed without reference to either Jesus of Nazareth or the Christian Church. They even began to wonder whether they should not acknowledge the fact that the God of Israel is also active in Christianity and that the Christian claim to being children of Abraham cannot be dismissed as being presumptuous.

Such awkward moments motivated our decision to come together not only for political reasons, but also for the sake of God, allowing God, as ruler of the kingdom of Heaven, to take us together into his service. The results of our reflections were published in 1979 in a paper entitled "Important Theological Issues in Jewish-Christian Dialogue," which was credited as being one of the best statements about the relationship between Judaism and Christianity.

3. The problem of Christianizing the Jews

Two years later a Jewish member of the discussion group, Dr. Edna Brocke, challenged us by asking: "Although we appear to understand each other well, I can't help feeling that you're not really telling us everything, that you still have a trump card in your pocket. What I would like to know is: what, in the end, do you hope for us? About what do you pray to God when you think of us? Do we have to believe—at least at the end of time—that Jesus is the Messiah after all?"

It is well known that in the Middle Ages a cross was held before the Jews; if they refused to believe in it, that is, if they opposed forced conversion, they had to pay for it with their lives. The delicate topic of "Christianizing the Jews," which is no longer supported by any Roman Catholic group, was the central theme of a closed conference at the Walberberg monastery near Bonn. The papers read at this seminar were published under the title "Witness and Dialogue."

During the controversial exchange of opinions our Jewish partners admitted that Franz Rosenzweig's often-quoted phrase, "Whether or not Jesus was the Messiah will become apparent when the Messiah comes," releases and at the same time increases the strain on Christian-Jewish dialogue. But we all agreed that the ambiguity of the remark should not be interpreted to mean that Jews and Christians should postpone discussion about the hope of inheriting the kingdom of God—which unites them—and about the coming of the Messiah—which divides them—until the "Last Day." Jews and Christians have the right to listen to each others' testimony of faith, and to reflect on it before God, even if they are unable to approve of it. At the same time, it is their duty to give an account of their own hope without mistakenly interpreting that unconditional testimony as a hidden attempt at conversion.

The Christian partners admitted that the familiar expression, "We know the Messiah—you do not," puts a strain on religious dialogue, since it is not a question of knowledge versus ignorance here, but of one faith versus another. We agreed that it was our task to testify and give an account of our reason for hope, and that we could safely leave it to God to decide how to resolve the conflict, or contest, between the Jewish and Christian faiths. Well-meaning proposals as to the nature of a unification between Israel and the Christian Church would, so it seemed to us, hinder rather than assist God in his decision. For whatever the appearance of such a utopian system, would it not be a nightmare for the Jewish minority, even "under a Jewish flag"? Just as extermination can cause death, so indeed can being embraced, where the smaller partner could disappear in the arms of the larger.

4. The Ten Commandments as a foundation for human ethics

If, during the course of the group's later discussions, the main emphasis was on ethics, it was not meant to evade difficult issues or to be an eager attempt at discussing a topic of current relevance. On the contrary, Jews and Christians believe that God and God's historical actions are the force that determines everything in life, and that each life proves its worth in serving both God and God's creation. At first the question of the Jewish-Christian contribution to a meaningful life and the survival of humankind in our unstable world was discussed in detail with Jewish scholars in a two-day seminar at the Van Leer Institute in Jerusalem during our second journey to Israel in 1981; this discussion was expanded in an international debate among experts in Simpelveld, Holland, in 1983. The conference, which was also attended by Emanuel Levinas, Michael Wyschogrod, and Emil Fackenheim, was entitled, "So That the Earth Might Remain Human."

The excitement caused by the chosen theme arose from the conclusion that the decisive stumbling block in the three most important questions concerning humankind, namely justice, peace, and the preservation of the creation, is not the scarcity of resources and the inadequate development of scientific-technical methods, but human beings themselves and their lack of humanity. The greatness of the human person created in

God's image and the incredible depths of evil to which the human being is capable of sinking, as demonstrated in our century by the unsurpassable horror of the *Shoah,* cannot be weighed against one another. Human ethics, we all agreed, can only be based on belief in the biblical God and commitment to the Ten Commandments. The biblical religions in particular should therefore feel committed to spreading this belief through dialogue and through working together with all people of good will.

5. Auschwitz—a problem for Christians, too

The discussion group was faced with the most delicate debate of all while reflecting on the questions of guilt, suffering, and reconciliation. We were virtually forced to discuss this problem because we were also strongly affected by the public discussion about President Reagan and Chancellor Kohl's 1985 gesture of reconciliation at the military cemetery in Bitburg. The use of the collective "we" for both Jews and Christians seemed to be in jeopardy in our group as well. It was not just a matter of religious identity and social commitment. Here we were talking about existence in the face of the suffering and death of millions, and about the responsibility faced for the dead. Since we felt a sense of joint responsibility for the public debate that took place fifty years after the *Reichskristallnacht,* the discussion group set themselves the task of preparing a declaration that led to almost everybody asking: "After fifty years, how can we talk about guilt, suffering, and reconciliation?" Thirty thousand copies just of the German version of the declaration were ordered.

It is not difficult, even for those not directly involved, to understand why the question of the *Shoah* and its macabre forerunner, the *Reichskristallnacht,* became a real test for the discussion group: To forget cannot be the answer—to forget those murdered would be like agreeing to their death or declaring it to have no consequence; it is terrible to talk of the past as being "over and done with." Shall we forgive? That cannot be a solution either, because only the victims can forgive and they are no longer living. Reconciliation, shaking hands with each other, in spite of everything that has happened, is that perhaps a solution? Wouldn't reconciliation mean betraying the dead?

The asymmetry of our relationship compelled us to discuss our differences with *untrained* delicacy, to avoid demanding too much of each other. The *Shoah* certainly concerns us all, each of course in a different way: the offender and the victim, the perpetrators and those who looked away, the people living then and those living today. To illustrate this with an example: due to the horror of Auschwitz, many Jews lost their faith in humankind and even in God, as did their relatives and descendants. But, as our partners were quick to point out, on no account can this mean that Auschwitz is only a "Jewish problem": you as Christians must also come to terms with Auschwitz. Haven't the perpetrators lost their own dignity, and are they not thereby victims of their own atrocious deeds? All this must also concern the new generation, for it cannot be denied that, to quote Klaus Hemmerle, "my own folk were responsible." Another example: the historians in our group asked: "Who are we to judge the deeds of our ancestors? Who can say that we would have behaved any better?" Although being just demands consideration of all reasons for taking or not taking part in the atrocities, listing exonerations should not lead to the conclusion, "We couldn't do anything about it." It would be impossible to live with such reasoning.

Comparison of a medieval Jewish penitential rite (Maimonides, *Hilchot T'shuvah*) with the existing rite of the Catholic Church helped us considerably in understanding the meaning of reconciliation and how it can succeed. The comparison showed us that Jews and Christians apparently have the same God who guides us in the same way toward conversion, repentance, and reconciliation. But even more helpful than such testimonies of our tradition was the personal witness from members of our group and from friends. I would like to illustrate the "miracle of reconciliation" with an episode that was significant for our work.

> During our trip to the United States in 1986 the Jewish theologian Michael Wyschogrod guided us through the Lower East Side of New York, the Jewish quarter. Together we went to a bookbinder. Before Wyschogrod could introduce us, the old shopkeeper shouted from behind the counter: "Get out, Nazis, murderers!" Any attempt to appease him was in vain. But only half an hour later we were standing around old Rabbi Singer, who had guided us round a ritual bath *(Mikweh)*, and we were smiling because of his Yiddish idiom. Afterward, when we expressed how moved we were by his wisdom and kindness, our friend Wyschogrod answered: "I wanted, for once, to show you a holy man." Half an hour later, in view of what we had just experienced, we asked

> him over lunch: "Do you think reconciliation is possible?" He answered: "I will give you a personal answer to this personal question. As I looked at your group around Rabbi Singer I saw again, as if it were yesterday, the grinning faces of the German soldiers in Warsaw as they stood round a small, defenseless rabbi, maliciously ill-treating him. I know I am doing you grievous wrong with this comparison. But as long as I cannot rid myself of this association, I cannot imagine being reconciled with you." We asked: "What can we do?" He answered: "Just carry on with what you are doing! And please give me time!" Shortly afterwards Wyschogrod did actually try to clarify what had happened with the bookbinder. We summed up our New York trip as follows: in view of the difference between being unreconciled, on the way to reconciliation, and being already reconciled, may we presume to pass judgment on those involved, or even play Christian forgiveness off against Jewish reluctance to be reconciled? Would it not be better to endure the fact that our contemporaries all react differently and grant them the time they need to become reconciled? While we are still trying to come together, could we not already be joint witnesses and advocate reconciliation in our strife-torn world?

The presentation of our declaration, "After Fifty Years," and the subsequent discussion during an assembly of the Central Committee of German Catholics in the spring of 1988, when two Jewish members of the discussion group, Marcel Marcus and Ernst Ludwig Ehrlich, also took the floor, became an outstanding event in the long history of this most influential body of lay persons in Germany.

A few months later we were confronted anew with the *Shoah*. In order to contribute objectively to the public discussion in Germany, we submitted in 1990 a statement entitled "Convent and Cross in Auschwitz?" We Catholics asked our Jewish members: "What can be wrong about nuns in Auschwitz praying for those who died there and doing penance for the murderers?" The actual reason for their objection, even for them, took a while to be clarified. "Let the emptiness of this place of unbelievable horror and senselessness speak for itself, without trying to interpret it with a symbol, especially that of the cross, which is particularly burdensome for us. If a person is able to pray there, that is fine. The ability to pray there is always an incomprehensible wonder for us—but having a cloister there, a permanent institution, where, so it would seem, people may permanently live and pray as a matter of course—that is something quite different." We reflected deeply on this answer—not only out of respect for the feelings of our Jewish brothers and sisters, but also in order to ask ourselves: Would it not sometimes reflect more faith to endure difficult questions rather than to supply a "Christian answer"? Our 1993 trip to Poland and the confrontation with Auschwitz from a Polish point of view did, it would seem, present us with a new predicament.

6. Critical reappraisal of history

Jews and Christians are separated more by the long history of estrangement and hostility of the church toward Jews than by theology. Many of our recent discussions have revolved around this thesis, which has been dealt with for years in our group by Ernst Ludwig Ehrlich. In a position paper resulting from our discussions, entitled "Jews and Judaism in the new *Catechism of the Catholic Church*—an Intervention" (1996), we regret above all that the Roman catechism appears to be oblivious to history because, in most of the main topics on the Christian faith, "the Jewish element in Christianity" is not mentioned; in many sections the text appeared to us to be more non-Jewish than anti-Jewish. Four statements on our paper by our US-American dialogue partners show that the same discussion with a similar argumentation went on there. In response to the 1998 Vatican declaration about the *Shoah* we published "Reflections on the *Shoah*—the Catholic Church's Share of the Blame and Responsibility," in which we criticize the fact that, after our years of work, the church only managed to express a half-hearted apologetic admission of guilt. In spite of such critical comments, which were always linked with a positive appreciation, both the discussion group and the president of the Central Committee are convinced that relations between Jews and Catholics have developed well since the Second Vatican Council.

It might seem that the discussion group only reacted to events and statements in the universal church over the last few years. This is not the case. With two projects we made an important contribution to precarious problems of remembering and commemorating: in 1998 we published a thoroughly revised edition of the brochure, "A Journey to the Holy Land," and in 2002 the brochure, "Auschwitz: History and Remembrance." These are for Catholic pilgrims to Israel and for German-speaking visitors to Auschwitz respectively; their aim is not only to open up the provocative past and present of these places by means of texts and pictures, but also to invite people to contribute through discussion and testimony to a peaceful future. In both cases our group had to struggle with the difficulty that each name, each number, and each fact gave rise to emotions and controversy: Why mention the one and leave out the other? How do we do justice to the usually opposing views of Jews, Christians, and Muslims, of Poles and Germans, of Israelis and Palestinians? In the brochure on Auschwitz, how were we to present Edith Stein in an appropriate way? For many Christians she has become a bridge to the *Shoah* and to Judaism, but for Jews she cannot be a bridge to Christianity. Both these publications are unique in that they were written by Jews and Christians together, and for the brochure on Auschwitz, Polish partners were consulted by correspondence.

Our most recent project was a discussion of the document published by four American Jewish scholars, *Dabru Emet: a Jewish Statement on Christians and Christianity.* This document, written in the format of a short series of statements about the theological relationship between Judaism and Christianity, constituted the first major response by Jewish scholars to the new approaches by major Christian churches toward Judaism and the Jewish People since the *Shoah.* It seemed to the discussion group that the two hundred scholars from all streams of American Judaism were, in some way, responding to the 1979 statement made by our discussion goup that expressed the hope for a hand outstretched in friendship and collaboration. After some deliberations, the discussion group concluded that *Dabru Emet* rekindled the very same question that our group had asked twenty-five years ago: "What are the most important issues for the Jewish-Christian dialogue today?" It became very clear to us that the religious and social situation in Germany had changed in many ways since our first statement. We therefore decided to challenge ourselves and our readers with new points of view. Now we can offer our statement of April 2005 to our English-speaking readers and invite them to a deeper understanding of the Jewish-Christian dialogue in German-speaking countries.

As I survey the presentation of our work for a new audience, I would like to clarify one more point. During the past thirty-six years we had only two occasions where the topics we discussed were planned. Most of the others were virtually imposed on us by events. Our discussion group is not an organized research institute, but a changing group of people who are passionately interested in maintaining Jewish-Christian relations in lands that are experiencing the rebirth of Jewish life after horrendous destruction. We offer our work as a sign of guarantee that we Jews and Christians in Germany, Austria, and Switzerland are "coming together for the sake of God."

Documents

Important Theological Issues for Jewish-Christian Dialogue

May 8, 1979

I. Why Seek Dialogue?

1. Jews and Christians have a common ground for hope: the God of Israel who graciously turns toward humankind. Together they await the complete fulfillment of their hope: the definitive reign of God.

Because of what they have experienced of God and because of the world in which they live, Jews and Christians are challenged to give a common witness. They believe that the invitation to find life, a home, and peace in the Jerusalem of the life-giving God was addressed not only to them but to all peoples (cf. Isa 2:1-5; 60:1-22). As they themselves set out for this Jerusalem, where righteousness and faithfulness have their place (cf. Isa 1:26), they experience the obligation to pass on to all people the liberating power of their commitment to the God who can and wishes to grant life and a future (cf. Jer 29:11). God's call takes them into service for fashioning the world and makes them into people who prepare the way for hope, especially for those who have no hope. This call is, at the same time, judgment in that it frees them from any fixation on purely internal interests and fears. In following God's call, they are to become honest and courageous ministers of God's righteousness and advocates of God's mercy.

2. If the fact that Jews and Christians are bound together through the action of the God of Israel obliges them at all times to engage in dialogue,

the painful experiences of recent history place an even greater obligation on us to intensify and deepen this dialogue as far as possible.

- The past 1,900 years of the relationship between Judaism and Christianity have evolved as a history of growing apart, and the historical consequences of this were terrible. We also have to see the horrendous occurrence of Auschwitz, the attempt to destroy the Jewish people completely through Hitler's dictatorship, in this connection.
- In Judaism as well as in Christianity, both of which together owe their existence to the revelation of the God of Israel, there is a gradual awakening of a "spiritual" interest in one another. Jews and Christians acknowledge their common revelation precisely through this interest. Consequently, their interest in one another is in itself an act of worship of God.
- Jews and Christians must give a joint witness to a humanity whose very survival in humaneness is at stake. In this joint witness they must show and prepare concrete paths of righteousness and salvation.

II. Conditions of Dialogue concerning the Jew as a Jew and the Christian as a Christian

Because Jews and Christians transmit a common treasure of biblical writings as the basis of their lives, their dialogue has a foundation of inestimable value: faith in the saving and sanctifying God whose closeness to the patriarchs the Torah relates, and whose life-promoting teachings it proclaims. This is a hearkening to the God of the living and the dead, whose rule in the midst of the people, called by his name, the prophets announce. It is cleaving to the God who is both near and distant, whom the prayerful psalmists praise, and whose faithfulness they beseech even when everything seems to have been taken from them. It is faith in the creator God of whose goodness the proverbs and meditations of the sages remind us. To all of this Jews and Christians, in their respective ways, give testimony in their divine services and in their lives. But just here arises a typical difficulty for Jewish-Christian dialogue: Do the identical writings really provide the basis for a common life? To answer this question it is necessary to bear in mind some fundamental conditions of Jewish-Christian dialogue:

1. Without doubt, Jews and Christians will have to begin by working very hard together in order to come to a better mutual understanding. The images Jews have constructed and still construct of Christians, and the images Christians have formed and still form of Jews throughout history should be examined and corrected in an encounter in which each interprets his or her own journey for the other by going back to the common ground and in light of the common hope. And precisely in doing this, the one will not wait for the other to come and "study" them. Rather, each will feel the obligation to share what is his or her own. Conversely, for the sake of the common hope each one will develop an active readiness to listen to the other. By presenting themselves, in trusting one another and in revealing themselves to one another, both will be able to bear witness to that to which they know God has called them.

2. Jewish-Christian dialogue cannot succeed if Christians see in the Judaism of today merely a memorial of their own past—of the time of Jesus and the apostles. Similarly, the dialogue will not succeed if the Jewish partners see in the essential Jewish characteristics within the Christian faith nothing but the effects of a condition that existed in the past within the first Christian communities but no longer exists today. In both cases the one partner does not yet take the contemporary reality of the other seriously, but rather sees in the other nothing but a mirror of their own past. Contemporaneousness is the condition for every dialogue.

The Jewish partners cannot be satisfied if, in a conversation with Christians, they are seen merely as a surviving witness of the so-called Old Testament and the period in which the Christian communities originated. Conversely, the Christian partners cannot be satisfied if the Jewish partners think that only they have something to say to the Christians that is essential to Christian faith, while what the Christians have to say to the Jews is of no essential importance for Jewish faith. Based on the ecumenical experience of inner-Christian dialogue, we can draw confidence for the Jewish-Christian dialogue as well: there, too, both partners have learned the ability and the readiness to listen to the word of the other as a testimony about their relationship with God.

3. The very history that makes today's encounter of Jews and Christians more difficult can also open a path toward one another if that history is experienced and acknowledged as a truly common history that concerns us now—even if this can only be done partially at first.

When, in a prayer of the Easter Vigil, Christians ask that "the dignity of Israel" be bestowed upon all peoples, they cannot forget—they can at most suppress to their own detriment—the fact that the Israel of which they speak exists to this day and remains even until now the bearer of the "dignity of Israel." The Christian Church that calls itself "People of God" must not forget that the existence today of Judaism is testimony to the fact that, still today, the same God is committed in fidelity to the election through which he became Israel's God and through which he made Israel his people. That is why Christians today do not adequately understand their own dignity and election if they do not acknowledge or seek to understand the dignity and election of present-day Judaism. But in order to do this, they must get to know Jewish faith and Jewish existence through the testimony of their Jewish partners in dialogue.

If Jews rightly consider themselves to be "children of Abraham," they cannot forget—they can at most suppress to their own detriment—the fact that not only were the first Christians in the distant past children of Abraham, but, today as well, nobody can be a Christian without acknowledging Abraham as the "father of all who believe." Furthermore, the Jewish community is certain of the promise of the renewal of its covenant with God, as it is written: "Behold the days are coming, says the Lord, when I will make a new covenant with the house of Israel and the house of Judah, not like the covenant which I made with their fathers when I took them by the hand to bring them out of the land of Egypt" (Jer 31:31-32). The Jewish community must therefore not forget that there would never have been a community of Christians if these had not heard the call from the same God to enter into this "new covenant." That is why Jews do not completely understand how Abraham became the "father of a multitude of nations" (Gen 17) if they do not acknowledge or seek to understand the faith of today's Christians. But in order to do this, they must get to know Christian faith and Christian existence through the testimony of their Christian partners in dialogue.

4. Once the meaning of the historical bond between them has become conscious and been acknowledged, there is a possibility that both dialogue partners might let themselves be called to responsibility for one another. Each becomes a witness for the other to the mighty acts of God that are the reason for the one living today as a Jew and the other as a Christian. Both for Jews and for Christians a life of faith, a life out of the center of

existence, draws life from such a witness. And wherever the life of a community becomes a witness to God's saving action, this witness becomes precious, even irreplaceable for the other believer who lives out of the same salvific acts of God.

III. Central Themes of Dialogue

1. Companionship between Jews and Christians

The common goal of God's reign enables Jews and Christians to speak to one another from faith to faith. Both know that they have been called by God, both wish to respond with the love of all their heart, all their soul, all their mind, and all their strength to the will of God, which they have come to know through God's gracious election. Such agreement is important for common action in the world. But it is also important not only to acknowledge the fact of agreement but also to weigh the extent of this agreement. This is all the more so because precisely there, where our bond of agreement is most profound, the root of our disagreements is embedded.

For the Christian, the goal of God's saving reign, promised in Israel's Bible, is mediated through the Jew Jesus. Here already we can see not only the dividing but also the uniting function of Jesus: through the Jew Jesus, the Torah continues to be effective within Christianity. Through him the Torah as God's promise and command is given to Christians to be realized. Jews, on the other hand, do not first have to get to know Jesus in order to love the Torah; as Jews, they already have this love.

Of course, dialogue between Jews and Christians can only happen in a serious way when the Jewish partners also come with the assumption that God acted within Christianity in a way that concerns them "for God's sake"—even if they do not see in Christianity a way they themselves can or must go. That is why Christians ask whether the living presence of essential Jewish characteristics in Christian liturgy, Christian proclamation, Christian understanding of Scripture, and Christian theology does not make it possible for Jews to be interested in Christian faith and life in a way that goes beyond a mere acknowledgment of their existence from a distance.

On the other hand, Christians must grant to Jews that their interest in Christianity can be an interest "for the sake of the kingdom of heaven"—

even if it does not lead to their becoming Christian. The Jewish philosopher of religion Franz Rosenzweig (1886–1929) expressed one possibility for understanding Jewish interest in Christianity when he said: "Whether or not Jesus was the Messiah will become clear when the Messiah comes." Such an ambiguous way of putting it, of course, does not mean that Jews and Christians may put off their dialogue about the hope that unites them and about the question concerning the Messiah that divides them "until the Last Day."

Thus in reciprocal questioning some recognition of the salvific meaning of the other way can certainly be expressed. Jews can acknowledge that, for Christians, Jesus has become the way by which they find Israel's God. But they will make their appreciation of the Christian way dependent on whether the Christian faith in salvation given through the Messiah of God coming from the Jews diminishes their obligation to work in the service of justice and peace or confirms it. Christians understand Jesus as the fulfillment of the Law and the promise only if they follow him "for the sake of the kingdom of heaven," and in following him listen to his word: "Not everyone who says to me 'Lord, Lord' will enter the kingdom of heaven, but only those who do the will of my Father who is in heaven will enter it" (Matt 7:21).

Thus the reciprocal appreciation of the other's way is indivisibly linked with considerable differences in attitude toward Jesus and to the question whether or not he is the Messiah of God. However, this forces neither Jews nor Christians to do away with the fundamental unifying content of the one will of God that calls them. Consequently, on the basis of this very principle, it is forbidden for both Jews and Christians to try to move the other to become unfaithful to the call of God to them both. It is not forbidden for tactical reasons. Reasons based on humane tolerance and respect for religious liberty are also not the only considerations in this prohibition. Rather, the deepest reason is that both Jews and Christians know themselves to be called by one and the same God. Christians, on the basis of their own understanding of their faith, cannot refrain from testifying to Jesus as the Christ, even when they are with Jews. Because of their own understanding of who they are, Jews cannot refrain from emphasizing that the Torah has not been surpassed, even when they are with Christians. In either case this includes the hope that through this witness the others' fidelity to the call of God, which they have heard, might grow and mutual understanding might be deepened. Conversely, this should not include the expectation that the others might go back on or weaken their "yes" to their own call.

Christians believe that the Messiah promised in the Scriptures has come in the person of Jesus. The nearness of Israel's God is what familiarized them with Jesus as their brother and at the same time let them experience Jesus' love as God's own turning toward them. That is why it seems too little to them to regard Jesus merely as a shining example. Rather, they understand his life, death, and resurrection as a way by which God wants to lead all people to salvation. They see their belief in Jesus' love as offering room for all, confirmed in the fact that God has exalted him and so returned him alive. Thus what distinguishes Jesus from all who preceded him and from all that is human is not only a quantitative increase. Precisely the idea that what distinguishes Jesus is merely an increase in humanness would easily lead to the fatal conclusion that Christians are, after all, the better Israelites. A christology that professes Jesus as the incarnate Son of God does not need this kind of measuring. This christology is—perhaps only after painful experiences of its own—able to see communion with Jesus in the free "yes" of faith in him as the goal. This is true but at the same time they know that all those of whom God has grasped are given the possibility of an open and growing communion along the way. In this way Christians could give an acceptable meaning to the words of Rosenzweig quoted above.

Christians respond to the Jewish question whether the stringent commitment to the one and only God of Israel (cf. Deut 6:4-9) has not been betrayed through their profession of faith in the incarnate Son of God and their conviction in faith that it is precisely Jesus Christ who mediates to them and represents the one and only God of Israel. For Christians, God's becoming human in Christ is by no means a negation of the unity and uniqueness of God, but rather its confirmation. Indeed, God's becoming human presupposes that the one and only God of Israel is not an isolated God without relationships, but rather a God who turns toward humankind and who is also affected by what happens to human persons. As the Talmudim and Midrashim testify, this characteristic of God's is known to Rabbinic Judaism as well, albeit without reference to or connection with Jesus Christ. It goes without saying that Rabbinic Judaism also knows that the one and only God of Israel "dwells" not only in transcendence, but also in the midst of his people who suffer distress and persecution. He is their Lord, their Father, their Companion, and their Redeemer. Christian-Jewish dialogue about the living God of Israel is therefore a great sign of hope.

2. The Common Task

In spite of their disagreement in agreement, which is not glossed over, Jews and Christians are united in their calling to act and to bear witness together in the world. Some of the vital tasks they will have to face together for the sake of the future are, for example:

- In face of the mass murder of Jews and the attempted destruction of the Jewish people, how is it still possible to believe in God? How is it possible to bring guilt and suffering into the presence of God rather than suppressing or fixating on them? What does the systematic extermination of large segments of European Jewry and the founding of the state of Israel mean for Jews and Christians and for their encounter with one another? In view of the founding of the state of Israel as a central event in recent Jewish history, how is it possible to link the millennial hope in God's salvation with concrete political action in the present without succumbing either to ideologizing politics on religious grounds or politicizing religious faith?
- In a world that continues to be polytheistic (the gods are only called by other names today), what does it mean that Jews and Christians believe in one God? In a world in which wars are still essentially wars of religion (which becomes easily recognizable if we substitute the word "ideology" for religion), can and must Christians and Jews not develop jointly a critique of ideology that is grounded in revelation?
- In the face of world conditions that threaten the survival of humankind, do not Jews and Christians have the joint obligation to demonstrate and to show through example what the Bible understands by righteousness and freedom?
- One of the basic demands of biblical revelation common to Jews and Christians is unconditional respect for the life of the other. Jews and Christians should jointly specify what follows from this today in view of the dignity of the human person and of human rights. In

particular, for example, we need to develop a mutual ethics of the sciences, of technology, of care for the future. People who live after the year 2000 are also our "neighbors"!

- What concrete consequences can be drawn from the conviction common to Jews and Christians that the human person is created in the image of God? What obligations follow from the commandment of unrestricted love that is common to Jews and Christians (cf. Lev 19:18 and Mark 12:30)?

3. Reflecting anew on the controversy around law and grace

The encounter between Jews and Christians will also result in both sides having a clear perception of their reciprocal questions. Jews can convincingly reject the Christian reproach that they believe in "justification by works" only if they do not deny the danger that could follow from this attitude. They can do so all the more since they know that the warning against "justification by works" is part of their own religious tradition. The fact that the Torah makes a demand on the life of the person does not prevent that person's being dependent on God's mercy. Liturgical texts like those that characterize the celebration of the Day of Atonement, the most important feast of the Jewish year, can demonstrate this side of Jewish life to Christians in a very impressive way. Christians can convincingly reject the Jewish reproach that they suffer a "loss of ethics" only if they do not deny the danger that their hope in grace could result in their being tempted to neglect their responsibility for the world. They can do so all the more since they know that the warning against this danger is part of their own religious tradition. Church texts on the relationship between faith and works (cf. the Council of Trent), but also already Paul's admonition concerning "faith working through love" (Gal 5:6) are clear examples of this.

Jewish and Christian criticism of "justification by works," Jewish and Christian "rejoicing in the Law" (and the Christian joins in this rejoicing, as Paul expressly states in Rom 7:12) have a common goal: to maintain the ability to pray and to praise God. That is why Jews and Christians can only find their way to dialogue when they together acknowledge what is said daily in the Jewish morning prayer: "We do not rely upon our own righteousness, but on Your great mercy" (Dan 9:18).

IV. Postscript

The questions raised in this text seek to increase awareness of the fact that Jewish-Christian dialogue may no longer be left only in the hands of a few interested specialists. The topics mentioned here are at the center of both Jewish and Christian self-understanding. Over and beyond the encounter between Jews and Christians, they also have something decisive to contribute to the understanding of religions in general and to questions surrounding the future of humankind. That is why the discussion group "Jews and Christians" in the Central Committee of German Catholics calls upon all who are responsible for the initial and ongoing formation of priests and other pastoral associates, of teachers and of people responsible for education, as well as upon those responsible for adult education and for the media, and upon Jewish congregations and institutions to give more of their attention to these central topics of Jewish-Christian dialogue during the coming years and to make the public more aware of their importance.

After Fifty Years: How Can We Talk about Guilt, Suffering, and Reconciliation?

February 19, 1988

The desire to forget
prolongs Exile,
to remember is the secret
of redemption.[1]

Time is pressing

In November 1988 it will be fifty years since the day that was given the dismissive name *Reichskristallnacht* (Night of Broken Glass). The violent acts committed then were a further radicalization of the persecution of the Jews, which finally ended with the murder of six million Jewish men, women, and children. The sad result of the mass pogrom organized by the government during the night of November 9–10, 1938, was that nearly a hundred Jews were murdered, many were abused, and over thirty thousand were locked up in concentration camps. In all of Germany, synagogues and cemeteries were desecrated, set on fire, or destroyed; Jewish shops and living quarters were looted and demolished.

1. Quoted as a saying from Jewish wisdom in the speech given by President Richard von Weizsäcker on May 8, 1985, on the fortieth anniversary of the end of World War II. Published in: *Bulletin des Presse- und Informationsamtes der Bundesregierung* 52 (1985) 441–48. The saying is also written on the Yad Vashem memorial in Jerusalem, where it is ascribed to the Baal Shem Tov (ca. 1700–1760 C.E.).

Unlike the subsequent *Shoah*[2] in the extermination camps, these events happened in the sight of all. One not only could see them, one could not help seeing them! This is why today the old question assails us: how did people, and above all Christians, react to these events? There was much indifference and vileness, raw violence, systematic pillaging, and open rejoicing over damage done, but there were also signs of indignation, of sympathy, and of willingness to help.

We do not intend in this declaration to pass historical judgment on the behavior of those involved at the time. Why the churches did not then condemn what happened more clearly and distinctly, and to what extent this was due to the churches' insufficient awareness of their bond with the Jewish people, are questions that need to be worked on separately and are in urgent need of exploration. However, the fact that the churches did act as they did still afflicts the relationship between Jews and Christians. As members of the discussion group "Jews and Christians" in the *Zentralkomitee der deutschen Katholiken,* we are particularly burdened by the fact that the bishops remained silent at the time, for they were the only people who could still speak in public. Their clear and unambiguous rejection of Nazi racism,[3] renewed more than once, could have been concretized in this situation even though, and perhaps also precisely because, the church itself was in great straits. For them to take a clear stand it would have been sufficient to say a few simple words like those of the Berlin cathedral dean, Bernhard Lichtenberg: "We know what was yesterday. We do not know what will be tomorrow; but we experienced what happened today. Outside, the synagogue is burning. It, too, is a house of God."[4]

Even today, half a century later, we Jews and Christians are speechless before the incomprehensible horror of what happened during the Nazi

2. *Shoah,* derived from the etymological root that means "destroy, lay waste," is the Hebrew expression for the murder of the six million Jews. The word is more correct than Holocaust (biblically: whole offering).

3. The encyclical *Mit brennender Sorge,* which German bishops had suggested and had helped to write, and which was read from every pulpit on March 21, 1937, emphasized the incompatibility of the church's teaching with Nazi racism; on April 13, 1938, the Vatican called on all Catholic universities and theological faculties to combat the Nazi racist ideology; in August 1938 the bishops' conference in Fulda published a pastoral letter to the clergy "on the religious-ethical errors in the teaching on racism."

4. Hans-Georg Mann, "Bernhard Lichtenberg (1875–1943)," in Wolfgang Knauft, ed., *Miterbauer des Bistums Berlin. 50 Jahre Geschichte in Charakterbildern* (Berlin: Morus, 1979) 72.

regime. It is still difficult for Jews and Christians to overcome this inability to speak. In 1979 our discussion group took a necessary step toward new horizons in Jewish-Christian theological discussion and collaboration by publishing a declaration on "Theological Emphases in Jewish-Christian Dialogue."[5] This was and continues to be a helpful and sufficient basis for our theological discussion leading to a dialogue, of which "the essential and central aspect" should be "the encounter between today's Christian churches and today's people of the covenant concluded with Moses."[6]

But Jews and Christians are not only separated by theology. We feel, each of us in a different way, the burden of history. In our discussion group we also had to go through the painful experience of realizing that time alone does not heal wounds. We had thought that in fifteen years of Christian-Jewish dialogue we had learned how to think, pray, act, and live with one another. Nevertheless, we ourselves experienced the bitter controversy surrounding President Reagan's and Federal Chancellor Kohl's visit to the Bitburg military cemetery (which had been meant as a gesture of reconciliation) as a tearing open of old wounds. Not only in the wider public, but even in our midst, there was a wall of misunderstanding and irritation, which placed a very basic question mark behind the "we" of Jews and Christians in Germany. For a while some even felt that it was no longer possible for them to belong to our discussion group. Personal sharing and theological discussion within our group, as well as the speech given by our then president on May 8, 1985, and our encounter with American Jews during March 1986 in New York, helped us to break through to a new mode of talking together, a mode that has been purified by suffering.

During the last three years we Christians have realized anew that it is really a miracle when a Jew can grasp the hand stretched out toward him or her, after all the suffering and injustice inflicted on this people and on his or her relatives and acquaintances. Although many Jews were the first to extend their hands in reconciliation, others still have to learn to take this step, and to understand that reconciliation does not mean

5. In Zentralkomitee der deutschen Katholiken, ed., *Berichte und Dokumente* (Bonn) 39 (1979) 6–19.

6. Pope John Paul II in Mainz, November 17, 1980, during his encounter with representatives of the German Jews. In Rolf Rendtorff and Hans Hermann Henrix, eds., *Kirchen und das Judentum: Dokumente von 1945–1985* (Paderborn: Bonifatius; Munich: Kaiser, 1988) 76.

treason toward the dead. However, we Christians also have to learn that we can ask only for reconciliation, not for forgiveness, and that we can only ask for it and not demand it. If a Jew does not or does not yet feel able to fulfill our request, there are no grounds on which to press him or her, not even through well-meant "simple expectations." We must bear this lack of reciprocity.

In any case it is false to believe that time heals. Most wounds scar over, but they continue to be painful: however, "the *Shoah* is a deep wound that is still bleeding."[7] But this is no reason to let time pass by unused; for the later we begin, the harder it is to recognize the situation and to draw right conclusions from it.

These experiences made us recognize that our 1979 paper needs to be amplified; in particular, the question posed by the postwar generations about the kind and the degree of our responsibility—a question that has come more clearly to the fore—must be taken up so that it will become a basis for the encounter between German Catholics and Jews. More than forty years after the end of World War II we must still continue to work on the foundations of our encounter and to learn to be able to ask together: "How can we talk about guilt, suffering, and reconciliation?"

This is why, 50 years after the *Reichskristallnacht,* the discussion group Jews and Christians in the Central Committee of German Catholics worked out these theological reflections and entitled them: "After 50 years—How Can We Talk about Guilt, Suffering, and Reconciliation?"

Jews and Christians face a question

We Jews and Christians acknowledge a common testimony grounded in God's call: we "are caretakers and witnesses of an ethical system characterized by the Ten Commandments; in obeying these, the human person finds truth and liberty."[8] This testimony is important for the future of the world, and therefore we bear a common responsibility. "One of the great obligations of our day is to foster collaboration and shared thinking in this area."[9] However, again and again the burdens of the past get in our

7. *L'Osservatore Romano* (June 25, 1987) 1.

8. Pope John Paul II on the occasion of his visit in the synagogue of Rome on April 13, 1986, in: *Freiburger Rundbrief* 37/38 (1985/86) 5.

9. Ibid.

way when we want to tackle our tasks for the future. We simply cannot look to the future and in so doing ignore the past: for what happened in the past is the basis from which we must start; "whoever closes his/her eyes to the past, becomes blind about the present."[10]

And when Christians, especially Christians in Germany, only want to talk with Jews about the future, they make their partner suspect—often without realizing it and without wanting to—that their primary intention is to confirm that the past is over, that they want to be "unburdened," and not to return and draw nearer to the Jewish people through solidarity, understanding, and concern. Precisely because of this the burdens of the past remain as an unarticulated barrier between us and are all the more paralyzing. As long as the past is excluded there is only alienation, and no reconciliation. Unfortunately, part of the curse of evil is that the one upon whom wrong has been inflicted is often felt (and attacked) as an abiding reproach. The decision not to close our eyes to the past must come sincerely from our own heart, must flow from our own need: "The practical sincerity of our desire for renewal also depends on the acknowledgment of our guilt and on our willingness to learn painfully from our country's as well as our church's history of guilt."[11] We have to work on ourselves in order to be capable of this.

To refuse to learn from past guilt as well as to deny being affected are repressions; none of us can *not* be affected. We are caught up too deeply in guilt and suffering, with all their consequences. We must face this past guilt precisely by giving the guilt a concrete name; otherwise we are easily in danger of hiding anonymously behind a general acknowledgment of guilt.

For there is guilt and guilt, discovered or hidden, admitted or denied. There is the guilt of having done something evil and that of not having done something good, the guilt of the inhuman deed and that of the refusal to be a fellow human being. There is help granted and the omission of help, shouting with others and keeping silent.

Similar to guilt, suffering is also many-sided, be it physical or psychological. There is the suffering of those who did not escape and that of

10. Richard von Weizsäcker in his speech on May 8, 1985, p. 443.

11. The German Synod's Declaration on Hope. "Unsere Hoffnung," IV,2 in *Gemeinsame Synode der Bistümer in der Bundesrepublik Deutschland, Offizielle Gesamtausgabe* (Freiburg: Herder, 1976) 1:108.

those who left someone behind; the suffering of those who had to watch helplessly and that of those who, being born after the event, suffer in the second generation. There is also the suffering of those who recognize their guilt and desire forgiveness and reconciliation as well as the suffering of those who want to forgive but cannot.

To learn from the history of guilt means to accept and bear sorrow. We share the grief—sorrowing over what happened to us, our guilt, our suffering. We mourn the people and communities that were murdered and annihilated, the Jewish culture in Germany and in the rest of Europe that was destroyed, and the faith in our fellow human beings that was almost taken, especially from us Jews.

However, what weighs above all on us Christians is the awareness of the devastation that previous guilt toward the Jews has caused between our communities. This derives from evil and will lead to further evil if it is not counteracted. To overcome it remains the task of all who are affected in various ways: those who are directly guilty, if they are still alive; those who were contemporaries at the time and who carry within themselves the unpaid debt of their entanglement in the terrible events, even if they themselves committed no crime; and those who were not even born at the time or who were children and who nevertheless are called upon to accept liability for something they themselves did not do.[12] For we hope that they, too, will help to lower the mountain of estrangement and enmity that has grown up between us.

Return and repentance as understood by Jews and Christians

This is why our discussion group is constantly confronted with the question: "How can we bring guilt and suffering before God instead of repressing them or becoming fixated on them?" Because of our faith, we have the hope that this is possible, for we trust in a God who has the power to forgive and to overcome wrongdoing, who not only demands

12. "The burden of history remains—our common responsibility for the past remains. During these days we are often involuntarily reminded of this. But we should also think of this of our own accord. Not in a self-tormenting passion, to which we Germans tend all too easily, but in honest, sober reflection. This is also our task as Christians." Hans Maier in Generalsekretariat des Zentralkomitees der deutschen Katholiken, ed., *Der 8. Mai 1945 und die deutschen Katholiken* (Kevelaer: Butzon und Bercker, 1985) 21.

repentance of the human person but also offers it to him/her. "When we come to God as sinners seeking our salvation, the call to return is already effective in us. Return is . . . the path to joy and freedom as God's children that is opened up to us sinners."[13] Our discussions about how we handle suffering and guilt have shown that what we have in common is not limited to biblical foundations. We learned that our penitential guidelines, as interpreted by our respective traditions today, can bring us together too.

We have worked on what we can say together. We have discovered that Christians can fully affirm and experience what Jews say about guilt, suffering, and forgiveness without feeling that anything is lacking. In doing so, we Christians do not ignore the fact that we find repentance and renewal only through Christ and in communion with God. Nevertheless, we Christians do not know any mode or measure of forgiveness and reconciliation, of longsuffering and courage different from the one the Jews know. And it was not our task to discuss differences in teaching. Our goal is reconciliation in encounter. Thus our rootedness in Jesus Christ, precisely when reflecting on guilt, repentance, and reconciliation, does not hinder us in recognizing that we share, because of our roots, with our Jewish partners in dialogue a deep agreement in the matter itself. We consider this congruence to be a solid bridge to real encounter. We hope to contribute thereby to that area of dialogue, which the Pope characterized as its most important one.[14]

However, this congruence caused us to think further about our "penitential guidelines," which concern themselves with the individual, and to reflect further on them in regard to the historical and social dimensions of our guilt and suffering due to the Hitler dictatorship. It was precisely the fact that our different religious traditions agree profoundly about trusting in God's coming to meet us that gave and gives us strength and hope, for it is this first step of God's that alone makes repentance possible, a repentance, however, that is more than wishful thinking and demands of the human person that he/she really strive toward this goal with all his/her strength.

13. The German Synod's Declaration on Sacraments: "Schwerpunkte heutiger Sakramentenpastoral," C 3, in *Gemeinsame Synode der Bistümer in der Bundesrepublik Deutschland, Offizielle Gesamtausgabe* 1:261.

14. Cf. Pope John Paul II in Mainz, p. 152.

Having thus come to the conviction that essential elements and principles of our different traditions can help us to recognize what we should do and to what we should bear witness, we have tried in the following to continue the lines of thought of the Catholic penitential guidelines[15] and the Jewish "Laws of Repentance" *(Hilchot T'shuvah),*[16] which are both results of each tradition's specific understanding of the biblical message, and to develop out of them propositions that can show us the way toward reconciliation between Jews and Christians.

Traditional teachings and the new dimension of the problem

The penitential guidelines and *Hilchot T'shuvah* aim at helping persons to recognize the wrongs they have done, to work through their guilt, and to overcome their estrangement from God. It is our task now to recognize these essential elements and principles in our different traditions, which are valid and important for us today in regard to the problem with which we are concerned.

However, our theological teachings are challenged beyond their capacity when faced with the uniqueness of the event of the *Shoah.* Our traditional theological concepts are inadequate in this context because, on the one hand, what happened is beyond any imagining; on the other hand, the problem is not only one of overcoming the guilt of an individual in his/her relationship to his/her own community, but rather also the enmity that has grown up between the communities. The penitential guidelines and *Hilchot T'shuvah,* however, concentrate more on the personal guilt of the individual. It is rightly said that guilt, "like innocence, is not collective, but personal."[17] Nevertheless, the evil deeds of individuals often leave deep traces in the life of the community of which they

15. Cf. *Die Feier der Buße nach dem neuen Rituale Romanum. Studienausgabe* (The penitential rite according to the new Rituale Romanum) (Freiburg: Herder, 1974). Even though this rite is a consequence of Vatican Council II, it does not replace, but rather develops what was contained in the traditional penitential rite. Cf. also the decision of the German Synod, "Schwerpunkte heutiger Sakramentenpastoral" C, and also Deutsche Bischofskonferenz, ed., *Katholischer Erwachsenen-Katechismus. Das Glaubensbekenntnis der Kirche* (Kevelaer: Butzon und Bercker, 1985) 1:363–72.

16. The traditional Jewish teachings on remorse, penitence, and return were collected, among others, by Moses Maimonides (1135–1204) in his *Mishneh Torah* and entitled *Hilchot T'shuvah* (Laws of Repentance). His work is still authoritative today.

17. Richard von Weizsäcker in his speech on May 8, 1985, p. 443.

are members or for whom they act. We cannot, on the one hand, profess our membership in a community, and on the other hand evade co-responsibility for what was done or not done in the name of that community by pointing out our own innocence.

Whoever sins against a fellow human being sins at the same time against God and alienates himself or herself from God. Then to return to God is not possible without turning toward the fellow human person who has been offended, damaged, or defamed. For: "The Day of Atonement atones for the sins of the human person against God; the Day of Atonement does not atone for sins of the human person against his/her fellow human being until the latter's forgiveness has been attained,"[18] and the directive of Jesus is similar: "when you are offering your gift at the altar, if you remember that your brother or sister has something against you, leave your gift there before the altar and go; first be reconciled to your brother or sister, and then come and offer your gift" (Matt 5:23-24). But the sinner also sins against the community of which he/she is a part and alienates himself or herself from it. That "sin, through which the individual sins against God . . . (is) always also a sin against the ecclesial community, which suffers from it"[19] applies not only to sins against God in the narrower sense; for sins against our neighbor are also sins against God. Full reintegration into the community is therefore supposed to give the penitent the confidence that he/she has also been accepted again by God. But this is again true primarily as regards the individual sinner who is accepted again by his/her community. We, however, are confronted with the sin of one community against another, and that one, the Jewish community, had just begun to hope that, after previous persecutions and disparagements, it would now finally be respected and gradually accepted. The wrongs of individuals against individuals are embedded within the greater whole of the wrongs of one community against another. And "we all, whether we are guilty or not, whether we are old or young, must accept the past . . . are affected by its consequences, and bear liability for it."[20]

18. *Mishnah Yoma* VIII, 9. Similarly, this is also true of the penitential rite, *Die Feier der Buße nach dem neuen Rituale Romanum.* Pastorale Einfuehrung Nr. 18, p. 19: The act of penance "can consist in prayer, self-denial, and above all in serving one's neighbor, so that the social dimensions of sin and forgiveness may be made visible."

19. The German Synod's Declaration "Schwerpunkte heutiger Sakramentenpastoral," C 2, p. 260.

20. Richard von Weizsäcker in his speech on May 8, 1985, p. 443.

Therefore what we need in order to overcome the evil in the community is not only the consciousness of "collective shame,"[21] but also the willingness to accept liability,[22] to bear, along with others, the burden that weighs on the community. For we also read: "In addition, people often sin together. But they also help one another when they do penance."[23] In the good, as in the bad, a person is affected by the deeds and behavior of his/her community. This is not only true for the generation of those "who were there," but for everyone of whose history the *Shoah* is a part. This is why we all speak as people who are affected and concerned, why we can and may speak only as such, and why we do so in the hope that "penance always also (leads) to reconciliation with the brothers and sisters to whom damage is done through sin."[24]

Prior to full atonement and return to God, forgiveness from the person against whom the sin has been committed is required—not, however, before beginning the process of atonement, which is the prerequisite for forgiveness. There is no return to God without a wholehearted turn toward the person against whom one has sinned. We must obtain forgiveness from him/her, though we cannot demand it. However, the big problem is that for sins between individuals we can really only forgive the suffering that has been inflicted on us, and to the extent that it happened to us; conversely, we can really only ask for forgiveness for ourselves for the deeds and omissions of which we ourselves are guilty and to the extent that we are guilty.

A person can only forgive the sin and suffering inflicted on him/her; the individual can only ask for forgiveness for the sin he/she committed. This is particularly significant in our situation—of which President Herzog rightly said: "Only the dead have the right to forgive, and the living are not permitted to forget."[25] This is not a renunciation of the obligation and willingness to be reconciled, but rather the expression of a great awareness and maturity: the survivors and those who were born after the people murdered in Auschwitz have no authority to speak for the dead. Martin

21. Theodor Heuss, "The Courage to Love," speech given on December 7, 1949. In Hans Lamm, ed., *Theodor Heuss: An und über Juden* (Düsseldorf and Vienna: Econ, 1964) 122–23.

22. Richard von Weizsäcker in his speech on May 8, 1985, p. 443.

23. *Die Feier der Buße nach dem neuen Rituale Romanum.* Pastorale Einfuehrung Nr. 5, p. 12.

24. Ibid.

25. President Chaim Herzog on April 6, 1987, in Bergen Belsen.

Buber's utterance: "What am I that I could presume to forgive here?"[26] expresses neither a desire for vengeance nor a refusal to be reconciled, but rather a deep respect for the dead; not a refusal to forgive, but rather a rejection of what would be a presumption. This Jewish testimony can call Christians to reflect anew on their understanding of forgiveness.

Therefore, as helpful as the traditional teachings on repentance and penance are, for the reconciliation between Jews and Christians we cannot avoid the realization that the traditional modes of behavior must be reconsidered in a new and deeper way in order to apply them to the wrong for which one community as a whole must assume responsibility toward another community to whom, as a whole, wrong has been done. This is precisely where a lot of theological thinking has still to be done.

Steps in repentance

The stations in the process of reconciliation with God are remorse, admission of guilt and responsibility, the attempt to make reparation, the request for forgiveness from and reconciliation with the person to whom damage was done: "One must appease him/her and beg him/her to forgive . . . however, a person should not be stubborn by refusing to be appeased. . . . If one is asked to forgive, one should do so gladly and wholeheartedly."[27] The request for and the granting of forgiveness must be sincere, "wholehearted." All of us, Jews and Christians, must work on ourselves in order to be able to do this. Forgiveness that is granted too quickly, lightly, and in fact insincerely, does not lead to reconciliation, but only to repression among all concerned; and it damages everyone. But above all, in our relationships with human beings it is true to say: "No one can speak for God; no one can speak for others. Almost every Jew in Germany has had many people come to him/her and ask for forgiveness. What can he/she say? May he/she speak for the six million dead? May he/she speak for the Sinti-Roma, for the homosexuals? May he/she

26. 1953 in the Pauluskirche on receiving the Peace Prize, quoted by Albert H. Friedlander, "Begegnung nach 40 Jahren," *Der Monat* 297 (1986) 16.

27. Moses Maimonides, *Hilchot T'shuvah* 2:9/10. Cf. also the answer given by Jesus to Peter's asking how often one must forgive one's brother or sister: "Not seven times, but seventy-seven times!" (Matt 18:22).

even speak for Judaism, for the Jewish people living scattered all over the world, and may he/she say: 'You have been granted forgiveness!'? No."[28]

"If he/she has made him-/herself guilty, he/she should acknowledge the matter in which he/she has sinned" (Lev 5:5; cf. also Num 5:6-7). Before forgiveness is asked, guilt must be acknowledged, not as a mere lip service but as an articulated acceptance of guilt. "One must confess one's sins with words and say the things one has decided upon in one's heart,[29] for "through confession the human person acknowledges his/her sinful past, he/she assumes responsibility for it."[30] Even though, on the one hand, "the confession of guilt (. . .), seen even in a purely human way, has a liberating and reconciling effect (. . .) and at the same time the person making the confession opens him-/herself anew for God and the church community, thus gaining a new future,"[31] on the other hand, the passive acceptance of guilt is insufficient to work through that guilt and to gain atonement. Rather, it is necessary to enter actively into the past, to seek the causes not in an apologetic but in a truth-seeking way, and to be willing to express anew one's own guilt and that of previous generations in light of the new insights gained. We must work on our guilt (as on our suffering and our sorrow), and that means above all that we must try patiently to find the factors that led to our condition.

"After I had returned, I repented . . ." (Jer 31:18 [19]). The human person is changed by his/her return to God, for he/she can only return to God when he/she becomes aware of his/her distance from God and of the guilt that brought it about. Return leads to remorse, and remorse to return, and in this reciprocal process of atonement we again draw nearer to God. We may and we must rely on God's will for atonement, but precisely because we put our hope for full atonement in God, the process of atonement can never be completed for us. Atonement cannot become our "property," of which we can dispose. The more we experience the gift of atonement, the more deeply we understand that it is not something to which we have a claim. This is true of atonement with God and of reconciliation with our fellow human beings. And because the path of return is marked by dependence on each other we can experience full atonement

28. Albert H. Friedlander, "Begegnung nach 40 Jahren," 28.

29. Moses Maimonides, *Hilchot T'shuvah* 2:2.

30. *Katholischer Erwachsenen-Katechismus* 1:370.

31. Ibid.

in a concrete place and at a certain moment in time; at the same time we must continue to ask for it and struggle for it. The result is that this process is surely not possible when it is sought simply in order to be absolved from the burden of guilt feelings.

The return to God is linked to our turning toward the person who has been damaged. The effort to make reparation may not be seen as something one wants to get over with like an unpleasant burden. Rather, it must arise from remorse: it may not be simply a means of obtaining forgiveness; it is not rendered unnecessary through forgiveness and it cannot be limited to a certain period in time. Satisfaction is intrinsically linked to the penitential process itself—it is its "concrete realization"[32]—and even if we cannot "repair" what was done by human means, nevertheless pain can be "alleviated" in the present and "made better" in the future, and thus at least the "curse of the evil deeds" can be broken.[33]

Thus human forgiveness and reconciliation also depend reciprocally on the process of atonement with God. Their prerequisite is the willingness to go out to meet one another and thus also to try to imitate the example given by God. Both must go out to meet one another; both must find the way to each other again. To do this, we Jews must find our faith in our Christian fellow human beings again. And to make this possible for us is part of reparation, as it is part of the sin that many of us were robbed of this faith; for the "Holocaust . . . almost destroyed the awareness of a common humanity between Jews and non-Jews."[34] Not only Christians, but Jews as well must learn to shake hands with the other and to take hold of hands that are stretched out timidly, since the reconciliation "between Jews and non-Jews (is) a mental and spiritual life necessity for the Jewish people,"[35] for "Two people, both with one past, cannot in

32. The German Synod's Declaration "Schwerpunkte heutiger Sakramentenpastoral," C 7, p. 265.

33. Cf. Ernst Simon, *Das Zeugnis des Judentums* (Berlin, 1980), quoted from Albert H. Friedlander, "Begegnung nach 40 Jahren," 23: "The new Germany can only 'work through' or 'overcome'—whatever the expression may be—its most recent past if it is willing to do deeds of real return. Return means that, as far as possible, one causes the undoing of the consequences of the evil deed. No dead person is awakened to new life through return, but return can contribute to preventing new murders and wars."

34. Michael Wyschogrod, in Wilhelm Breuning and Hanspeter Heinz, eds., *Damit die Erde menschlich bleibt* (Freiburg: Herder, 1985) 81.

35. Ibid., p. 83.

the long run turn their backs on each other and ignore one another. It can mean something for humanity if this peace is considered and prepared and, God willing, ultimately attained in an honest way, and that also means: without forgetting."[36] ". . . there are transgressions that find expiation immediately, and others that can only be expiated after some time. . . ."[37] The length of time the process of atonement takes depends not only on the sincerity and urgency of the person seeking it and on the willingness and ability of the one forgiving; it also depends on the nature and gravity of the sin. "The act of penance and the amount of satisfaction must be in accordance with each individual person, so that he/she reestablishes order where he/she has disturbed it, and so that he/she receives a medicine appropriate to his/her illness."[38]

What we must do

Neither time nor forgetting heals our wounds. We will not come closer to one another by keeping silent. In that case all that happens is that the guilt of the one and the sorrow of the other burst forth over and over again as things that have been repressed, and they are not overcome. "There is no reconciliation without remembrance."[39] However, it is not enough that guilt not be forgotten; conclusions must also be drawn from it. After all, the fall of the criminal Nazi regime does not banish the danger of a repetition (wherever and by whomever). The abyss from which the sin arose is still present. Therefore we must be particularly attentive and sensitive in these areas.

The command to remember and not to forget is in no way a call to enmity. Neither is the willingness to forgive honestly and to be reconciled a betrayal of the memory of those murdered. But since the wrong done to the dead cannot be repaid by human beings, this human suffering may not become subject to a "natural" process of forgetting: "To forget would

36. Leo Baeck, quoted by Albert H. Friedlander, "Begegnung nach 40 Jahren," 18–19, who comments: "More than 30 years ago [Martin Buber and Leo Baeck] showed us a path. It was too early; and the path has still not been taken."

37. Moses Maimonides, *Hilchot T'shuvah* 1:4.

38. "Die Feier der Buße nach dem neuen Rituale Romanum. Pastorale Einführung 6," 14.

39. Richard von Weizsäcker in his speech on May 8, 1985, p. 443.

be treason: If we survived in order to betray the dead, it would be better if we had not survived."[40]

Our wounds can only be healed if the first steps *toward* one another can be followed by many steps *with* one another—steps with one another in the process of working on our sorrow and in the process of atonement, and then, reconciled, steps toward the future. There can only be healing when we can wait together for the kingdom of God, when we can work for it together and thus can "serve the Lord shoulder to shoulder" (Zeph 3:9). The will for this is a sign of hope and confidence and an expression of our trust in a God who forgives and who can also change the wrong that has been done. But atonement with God is something the members of a community cannot bring to fulfillment. That is why we human beings may not pass a final judgment, just as every desire to draw a line under past events prevents the development of really trusting relations.

40. Elie Wiesel and Albert Friedlander, *The Six Days of Destruction. Meditations towards Hope* (Oxford and New York: Pergamon Press, 1988) 47.

Convent and Cross in Auschwitz?

April 26, 1990

The facts

For the past five years the Carmel of Auschwitz has been a source of painful controversy between Catholics and Jews. During Pope John Paul II's visit to the Benelux countries in May 1985 an association known as *Kirche in Not/Ostpriesterhilfe,* which helps support the church in Eastern Europe, solicited donations with a pamphlet bearing the title "Your Gift to the Pope: A Convent in Auschwitz." The pamphlet referred to the existence of a convent of Discalced Carmelite nuns in the old "theater" building of the Auschwitz concentration camp. This structure, adjacent to the fence around the Auschwitz I camp, was where the Zyklon B poison gas was stored during the years of extermination and was part of the overall Auschwitz complex comprising Auschwitz-Birkenau (Auschwitz II), the extermination center three kilometers away, and several other camps.

The disclosure that the building houses a Carmelite convent evoked an immediate protest from the Jewish community, first in Western Europe and then in Israel and other parts of the world. Prominent Catholics, too, raised objections. In order to defuse the situation, senior Catholic and Jewish representatives met to discuss the matter. In a joint statement issued in Geneva on February 22, 1987, the two sides agreed to establish a Center for information, education, contact, and prayer outside the boundaries of the Auschwitz and Birkenau camps. The Center was also to be the home of the Carmelite convent. But although it was agreed that the project would be completed within two years, there were no signs of any action being taken.

After the two years had expired, the time limit was extended by six months. In this period there were still no signs of any steps being taken to build the Center and relocate the convent. In the autumn of 1988, however, a cross about seven meters high was raised in the convent's compound, opposite the place where Polish martyrs were murdered.

The controversy escalated in the summer of 1989 through the activities of local Jewish groups. The situation did not improve until the Vatican Commission for Religious Relations with Judaism endorsed the Geneva agreement on October 18, 1989. The tension was further eased when the Polish government called for an early solution to the problem. The fact that a plot of land has meanwhile been purchased is a hopeful sign.

Apart from relocating the convent and building the Center, it is necessary to clarify the differing Jewish and Christian interpretations of symbolism and spirituality, which are the real source of the conflict. This is the purpose of the following comment, especially in light of the debate on this problem in the Federal Republic of Germany.

Comment

No other name recalls Hitler's extermination camps more vividly than Auschwitz. Originally built to eliminate the Polish intelligentsia, it became the site where millions of people were murdered: Poles, Russians, Hungarians, Germans, Dutch, Belgians, French, Sinti and Romany "Gypsies," but above all Jews, merely because they were Jews. Unlike the other camps, Auschwitz, being the largest Jewish cemetery in Europe, symbolizes the *Shoah,* that is to say, the attempt to exterminate the Jewish people.

Especially in German-speaking countries, Auschwitz also stands for the catastrophe in Christian-Jewish history and exhorts a change in the Christian attitude. What the theologian Johann Baptist Metz said at the 1978 Catholic Convention in Freiburg is an obligation we Christians still have to honor: "We Christians can never go back beyond Auschwitz; but on closer examination, we are no longer able to go forward beyond Auschwitz by ourselves, only together with its victims."

This is why we in particular, Catholics and Jews who have been discussing our problems for the past twenty years, are saddened by the conflict that has arisen over the founding of a Carmelite convent in the Auschwitz extermination camp. Because promises have not been kept, it has damaged the credibility of the Catholic Church. At the same time, the conflict has strained the bond of unity within the Catholic Church. It has shown how heavy the burden of history weighs on us all, though, of course, in quite different ways on Christians and Jews. But we have also learned that our perceptions of each other's faith and way of life are quite different. It is difficult, therefore, to respect them and to take them seriously.

To the Jews among us, Auschwitz is the very place and name that stands for the *Shoah,* the manifestation of evil, of the incomprehensible silence of both God and human persons. It is no place for subsequent symbols or quick interpretations, for in the Auschwitz of today the reality of the past is present. Auschwitz is a tangible symbol. "One need only stoop to find the ash that fell from the sky at that time and scattered the wretched remains of thousands and thousands of Jewish children, silently and solemnly, into the four winds. On the soil of Auschwitz we can hear the voice of memory that burns but never dies away" (Elie Wiesel). If something is added as a symbol it may diminish the force of Auschwitz's message. The symbolism of Auschwitz has the most telling effect if it is kept free from additional symbols. This absence and avoidance of symbols also manifests a solidarity with all the victims, as explained by Theo Klein, head of the Jewish delegation to the official talks on the "Carmel" conflict. "We [Jews]," he said, "have never denied that Poles, Russians, 'gypsies,' and others died there. We do not insist that Auschwitz be made a synagogue. . . . [The dead] were Catholics and Protestants, Jews, Muslims, and freethinkers. None of these groups can claim an exclusive right to commemorate them."

Auschwitz must be protected from any group or institution laying claim to the truth and seeking to use Auschwitz for its own purposes. Our respect for those who suffered and died at Auschwitz, but also for the Jews as the people of God's covenant, forbids us Christians at this site to resort solely to our Christian forms of liturgy and spirituality. In exercising this restraint, the renunciation of symbols can be a positive sign. There are dimensions and depths of suffering—and of suffering in relation to God—that make silent abhorrence and reflection the appropriate response.

We Christians must appreciate the seriousness of the question non-Christians ask about our theology of the Cross, which has changed for us from a pillory to a token of redemption. Throughout history many non-Christians, especially Jews, have experienced the Cross as a symbol of persecution: through the Crusades, the Inquisition and compulsory baptisms, the pogroms and persecutions. Thus we must learn to realize that for many people the Cross means something quite different from the message we intend it to give. Our symbols, intentions, and criteria cannot serve as the standard for all others.

We Christians, too, can perceive the Auschwitz devoid of symbols as a symbol in itself. Its emptiness can serve as an eloquent reminder of the forsakenness, the lack of solace and the terror of the many who had to live and die there. A convent might cover up that emptiness. A cross erected there today could conjure up a Christian presence to a degree that was not there before. Those who ask what it is about Christian nuns praying and making atonement there that is so disturbing to the Jews must learn to understand that it is improper for us subsequently to adopt Auschwitz for Christianity or even give the impression of doing so. Prayer for the victims of Auschwitz is independent of the place Auschwitz; expiation for past atrocities is not tied to the place where they were perpetrated.

True, it is a tradition of Christian piety going back to the early history of the church to erect a cross or a church at a place of martyrdom or over the graves of martyrs. But that tradition cannot be continued at Auschwitz. It would seem presumptuous because the dead at Auschwitz are not "our" martyrs, even though there were men and women among them who died as Christians. Furthermore, it would distort the fact that it was baptized people who became perpetrators. However understandable the longing of Christians to place the abysmal suffering of Auschwitz under the Cross of Christ so that the light of hope from the Resurrection may radiate over this place of incomprehensible Godforsakenness and contempt for humankind; however great the seriousness with which the Polish people wish to make that site a symbol of their own martyrdom and renewal, Auschwitz must for all time be preserved as the place where millions of Jews died, abandoned by an indifferent world and by the churches, who, after all, live with the Jewish people in one and the same covenant of God.

We Christians must genuinely accept the burden of history. "For history is not something external; it is part of the church's own identity and can remind us that the church, which we profess to be holy and mysterious, is also a church guilty of sin that needs to stop and reconsider" (German-language Bishops' Conference marking the 50th anniversary of the pogrom of November 1938).

In memory of Auschwitz we Christians must understand

- that the murder of millions of Jews is so closely associated with the name of Auschwitz that the voices of the members of precisely *that* people must not be ignored when "deciding" about Auschwitz;
- that we have forfeited much of our credibility because, as religious communities, we at that time—in spite of the exemplary conduct of individuals—ignored the suffering of the Jewish people;
- that we must strive to change our attitude and renew our relationship with the Jewish people;
- that Auschwitz also stands between the Polish and the Jewish people and needs to be remembered as a place of Polish suffering;
- that—and this may be the most difficult of all—ours are not the only criteria, or the only appropriate ones, no matter how sincerely we consider them to be the true ones.

As Jews and Christians we are convinced that Auschwitz must not be allowed to become a place of superficial inspection or ideological instruction. It will not be easy to preserve it in such a way that it keeps alive the memory of the victims and to enable visitors to show respect in their own different ways. The proposed Center outside the camp should help achieve this aim. This undertaking and the transfer of the convent and the cross are necessary steps that can demonstrate the seriousness of the Catholic renewal in terms of the church's continuing affinity with the Jewish people (and with individual Jews) that, as Pope John Paul II said on visiting the great synagogue in Rome, began with the Second Vatican Council. It faces the test whether we Christians as the "church after Auschwitz" are prepared for and capable of turning back, of *T'shuvah.* This must be proved precisely at Auschwitz.

Jews and Judaism in the New *Catechism of the Catholic Church*—An Intervention

January 29, 1996

The *Catechism of the Catholic Church* was published in 1992. In the Central Committee of German Catholics the discussion group "Jews and Christians" examined the *Catechism,* concentrating specifically on the extent to which it gives expression to the efforts made toward achieving a new view of Judaism.

The *Catechism of the Catholic Church* is part of a centuries-long tradition of catechisms in the church. From time immemorial, Christians have found in the catechism a short summary of Christian teaching appropriate for their time. Priests and laity have formed their fundamental understanding of Christian life through catechisms. In local communities, schools, and families, catechisms were of great pastoral significance.

Today we can see that the treatment of Israel and Judaism in many of the catechisms that existed before the Second Vatican Council was inadequate. These catechisms displayed anti-Jewish tendencies, unjustifiably accused Jews, presented a distorted portrayal of the Jewish tradition and way of life in the Bible, and declined to take post-biblical Judaism seriously as an entity in its own right. These catechisms supported the Christian contempt for Judaism that has had such disastrous consequences.

In the Second Vatican Council's decree *Nostra aetate* of October 28, 1965, the Church redefined its relationship to Judaism, recalling the spiritual bonds between the two. Ever since, the church has been on the way to a better understanding of Judaism and to a renewed definition of its own relationship to Judaism. Among the important steps in this process were the "Guidelines for the Implementation of the Council's *Nostra Aetate* Statement, Article 4," published on December 1, 1974, by the Vatican Commission for Religious Relations with the Jews. The "Guidelines for the Correct Portrayal of Jews and Judaism in the Sermons and Catechesis of the Catholic Church," published by the same commission on April 26, 1985, moved in the same direction. Pope John Paul II showed a new esteem for Judaism in many addresses and when visiting Jewish communities during his pastoral travels.

The new *Catechism of the Catholic Church* may be different in content and form, in intention and audience from earlier catechisms, but this *Catechism* also is intended to be a "sure norm for teaching the faith," as well as a "sure and authentic reference text for teaching Catholic doctrine and particularly for preparing local catechisms" (John Paul II in the introductory *Apostolic Constitution*). Thus the significance of the new *Catechism of the Catholic Church* for the church of our time is not to be underestimated. The ongoing current discussion of the *Catechism of the Catholic Church* has pointed out not only its positive features, but also its weaknesses. Our discussion group also wishes to present a multifaceted critique on this topic.

It should be noted that when the *Catechism of the Catholic Church* explicitly discusses Judaism, it does not return to positions preceding the statements of the Council on Jews and the relationship of the church to Judaism. It is clearly stated that Jesus was a Jew and that he held the Torah in honor (423; 577). The Pharisees and Jesus' relationship with them are presented in a nuanced way (579; 595). In the paragraph entitled "The Relationship of the Church to the Jewish People" (839), the *Catechism of the Catholic Church* explicitly quotes the Council and mentions the irrevocability of the election of Israel (121; 839). Above all, it is explicitly stated that the Jews are not collectively responsible for the death of Jesus (597). Occasionally references are made to the significance of present-day Jewish life for a better understanding of the Christian liturgy (e.g., 1096). These and other statements are a hopeful indication of the earnestness with which the church wishes to renew its relationship with Judaism.

However, with regard to certain other important points the *Catechism of the Catholic Church* fails to fulfill current expectations and demands. An appropriate positive picture of Judaism as the older sister of Christianity is lacking. Love of God and of one's neighbor as the center of Jewish existence, regard for the Torah, the hallowing of God's name and the hallowing of daily life in post-biblical Judaism as well are not mentioned. Moreover, the *Catechism of the Catholic Church* fails to indicate the presence of things Jewish within Christianity. When reference is made to a Jewish presence within Christianity, it is done in such a way that Judaism loses its unique value or becomes simply a prefiguration of Christianity. The words of Pope John Paul II, on his visit to the great synagogue of Rome on April 13, 1986, seem to have been forgotten here: "For us, the Jewish religion is not an external phenomenon but belongs in some way to the internal reality of our religion. Thus our relationship with Judaism is different from our relationship with any other religion."

The living relationship between the church and Judaism could have been shown in all four sections of the *Catechism of the Catholic Church* (Creed, Sacraments, Ethics, Prayer). It is true that central contents of all four sections are developed from the "Old Testament," the Jewish Bible, as the irrefutable foundation of Christian belief and life, though this is done in very different ways from section to section. But these matters are not presented as common beliefs of Jews and Christians whenever that is the case. Thus, to name just a few examples, in the paragraphs on the doctrine of God there is no reference to the fact that faith in the one God (200), who is gracious and merciful (210–11), is also the faith of present-day Judaism. This was presented in exemplary fashion in the *Catholic Catechism for Adults* published by the German Bishops' Conference in 1985 (63; 75). One also looks in vain for a reference to Judaism in the statements about the Decalogue and the Commandment of Love (2055). The relationship between the "Our Father" (2765) and the Eucharist, on the one hand, and current Jewish prayers and feasts, on the other, is scarcely hinted at.

The *Catechism of the Catholic Church* obviously finds it difficult to recognize post-biblical Judaism as an independent entity next to the church in the history of salvation and, in particular, as the people of the covenant that was never revoked by God. This is less obvious in paragraphs dealing specifically with Judaism than in paragraphs dealing with the church, where the Catechism speaks as if Judaism did not exist, even though such reference would be necessary from the very nature of things.

When the *Catechism of the Catholic Church* does speak of the relationship between Judaism/Israel on the one hand and the church on the other, its language often becomes oscillatory and its theology contradictory. There are passages that come close to the position that was retracted by the Council: that the church as the "new," authentic people of God has replaced the "old" people of God (674; 761–63). On the one hand the *Catechism* claims with the New Testament that Israel's vocation is irrevocable (839), but in other passages it appears that the covenant with Israel has nevertheless been severed and has been replaced by the new and eternal covenant of God in the church (762). Furthermore, the fact that the *Catechism* makes the coming of the glorified Messiah dependent on the recognition of Jesus by the whole of now "hard-hearted" (Rom 11:25) Israel is difficult for Jewish self-understanding to accept, because it makes Jews bear responsibility for the beginning and the delay of eschatological time (674).

There are three areas in particular where the *Catechism of the Catholic Church* does not succeed in wholly implementing the will of the church for renewal. Here deficiencies that were already present in earlier catechisms still endure.

1. The relationship between the two Testaments of the one Christian Bible remains unclear and ambiguous. On the one hand the value of the revelation of the "Old Testament" as such is repeatedly reinforced (121–23; 129). On the other hand it is continually relativized. This is due above all to the fact that the Old Testament, with help from a typological method of interpretation contrary to its own intrinsic value (121), appears predominantly as an incomplete early draft ("typos") that finds its fulfillment only in the New Testament. According to this "typology" what God says in the Old Testament is entirely directed toward the New Testament and achieves its definitive form only there (140). This is clear, for example, in the way certain important themes are presented. Here we can only mention them briefly: the prophetic promises of love have been fulfilled in the new and eternal covenant (2787); the execution of Jesus announces the destruction of the Temple of Jerusalem (586); the literal sense of the ancient Jewish Law is the "severe pedagogue" (Gal 3:24) directing Israel toward Jesus (708); the Law is preparation for the Gospel, which offers the New Testament "types" to illustrate the new life according to the Spirit (1964); the Jewish exile stands in the shadow of the Cross and the "holy

remnant" that returns from exile is a figure of the church (710). When Augustine is quoted as saying that "the New Testament is hidden in the Old, and the Old is revealed in the New," theological reflection on this is lacking (129; 2763). Necessarily this kind of typology must result in depicting the Hebrew Bible as the imperfect predecessor of the New Testament. In the *Catechism of the Catholic Church,* typology holds the two Testaments together. Therein lies the danger that the history of biblical Israel and the memory of this history, which is constitutive for Judaism, could disappear. Therefore typology, as it is used here, can be a milder form of the disinheritance of Israel that the church has long since repudiated in other documents.

2. The church's anti-Judaism is not addressed. Its roots lie in the separation of the early church from Judaism and the consequent anti-Jewish polemics that are already present in the New Testament. Through some earlier catechisms this anti-Judaism became widespread in the church. The omission of such an issue is hard to understand today. A catechism published after the *Shoah* should have acknowledged the sinful history of previous catechisms, should have named the effects of this history, and should have drawn the necessary consequences from this.

3. The *Catechism of the Catholic Church* does not make use of the opportunity to present the renewed relationship between Jews and Christians as a sign of hope in the midst of a seemingly unredeemed world and as a challenge to work, both together and separately, for the coming of the reign of God.

As a summary we may remind readers of the 1988 declaration "After 50 Years—How Can We Talk about Guilt, Suffering, and Reconciliation?": "Our wounds can only be healed if the first steps toward one another can be followed by many steps with one another—steps with one another in the process of working on our sorrow and in the process of atonement, and then, reconciled, steps toward the future. There can only be healing when we can wait together for the kingdom of God, when we can work for it together and thus can 'serve the Lord shoulder to shoulder' (Zeph 3:9)."

Statements from USA

1. Eugene J. Fisher

First I would emphasize the significance of the Central Committee's statement that the *Catechism of the Catholic Church (CCC)* "does not retreat from the statements of the Second Vatican Council." The *CCC* is clearly not a document that could have been produced before the Council. Its intention is not to move forward the theological agenda in Catholic-Jewish relations (or any other field), but rather to consolidate conciliar teaching. Pursuing this goal it relies on and refers to subsequent teachings of the Church, such as the two documents of the Holy See's Commission for Religious Relations with the Jews (1974, 1985) cited in the statement of the Central Committee, as well as statements of Pope John Paul II. These documents, then, in turn provide an interpretative and I would say normative frame within which to understand the *CCC* itself.

In this context it is important to acknowledge that the *CCC* devotes not simply a paragraph to debunking the ancient canard of collective Jewish guilt for the death of Jesus, but an entire section developing the catechetical appreciation of Article 4 of the Creed itself ". . . suffered under Pontius Pilate, was crucified, died . . . ." Sections 574–598 provide an extended discussion of why the catechist cannot present "the Jews" as collectively guilty of the death of Jesus, culminating in the citation from the Roman *Catechism of the Council of Trent* made famous by Jules Isaac in his now classic works on "the teaching of contempt." Theologically, "all sinners were the authors of Christ's Passion," especially we Christians who sin knowing that this is so (598). The collective guilt canard was rightly identified by Professor Isaac and by *Nostra aetate* as the heart of the collection of invidious pronouncements on Jews and Judaism over the centuries. It is here dismantled at some length and put to rest.

Second, a number of the Central Committee's criticisms of the *CCC* cluster around its use of typology and fulfillment theology with regard to the relationship between the Hebrew Scriptures and the New Testament. It is quite true that an opportunity was lost here to tackle head on a set of theological difficulties that the 1985 *Notes of the Holy See* aptly called "the sign of a problem unresolved." But while the *CCC* does not resolve the problem, in my opinion neither should it be seen as inhibiting in any way the creative work of so many leading Christian and Jewish theologians who are at present grappling with it. Typology and fulfillment, in and of themselves, are not the problem. One can find typology in Jewish tradition and even within the Hebrew Bible. And "fulfillment" is a necessary theological statement in the New Testament and in Christian liturgy.

The problem, as I understand it, is the presumption that a typological or fulfillment understanding of the Hebrew Scriptures will necessarily preclude other understandings, such as the biblical critical, rabbinic, or even mystical understandings. The *CCC,* following the 1985 *Notes* and *Dei verbum,* clearly says it does not. The fact that the *CCC* does not embody this principle in its own uses of Scripture does not lessen the validity of the principle itself. We as Christians can and must learn to "profit discerningly," in the words of the 1985 *Notes,* from Jewish traditional and contemporary understandings of their Bible. It would be a mistake, in my view, to read the *CCC* as in any way closing the door on this crucial work of the dialogue and the effort to integrate the results of the dialogue into the "mainstream" of Catholic education at all levels.

I would quibble, therefore, with some of the phrasings in the Central Committee statement, such as the charge that because the *CCC* sees in biblical Judaism prefigurings of the events of the New Testament, therefore "Judaism loses its unique value or becomes simply a prefiguration of Christianity." Or again: "Necessarily this kind of typology must result in depicting the Hebrew Bible as the imperfect predecessor of the New Testament." This, of course, could happen if the only resource available to catechists were the *CCC.* But it is not. The statements of Pope John Paul II, the Holy See, and Bishops' Conferences around the world exist and remain official church teaching. The *CCC* did not intend to replace the normative teaching of the church, but rather to augment it and in a sense "package" it in a way exportable to many different cultures. It is not properly understood as a sort of doctrinal Code of Canon Law or even a modern *Summa Theologica.*

I would urge readers of this report also to consider the possibility of opening up the category of "fulfillment" to new understandings that will preserve what the kerygma of the gospels authentically means to teach while at the same time avoiding the danger that we know all too well from history of reducing fulfillment to supersessionism. The *CCC,* as the Central Committee acknowledges, clearly condemns supersessionism and honors the "irrevocable" nature of God's call to the Jewish people as God's own people. How is this to be articulated theologically and taught catechetically? While the *CCC* does not provide the answers to these great questions of our age, neither does it inhibit ongoing efforts by theologians and biblical scholars to resolve them.

One small example may here suffice. The statement of the Central Committee twice refers critically to paragraph 674 of the *CCC,* arguing that it "makes Jews bear responsibility for the beginning and the delay of eschatological time." Frankly, I found this paragraph to be rather more enigmatic. For while its initial reference to Romans 11:20-26 does appear to do just that, its concluding reference to Romans 11:12-25 does just the opposite. Following Paul, it places the responsibility not on the Jews but on the Gentiles: "The 'full inclusion' of the Jews in the Messiah's salvation, in the wake of the 'full number of Gentiles,' will enable the People of God to achieve 'the measure of the stature of the fullness of Christ,' when 'God may be all in all.'" How one interprets this passage, then, depends on how one understands Romans. For that the catechist will need to resolve the eschatological conundrum posed by Paul.

Finally, I would put on the record for readers of this report my own listing of what I see as the key catechetical principles to be derived from the *CCC.* It is important, I feel, to contemplate not only what might have been in our proverbial half-empty glass but also what is indeed in it.

Basic Catechetical Principles of the CCC *with Regard to the Presentation of Jews and Judaism*

It seems clear that the *Catechism* very explicitly intends to break with the major elements of the ancient "teaching of contempt" that envisioned God cursing and punishing "the Jews" for their alleged collective guilt in killing Jesus ("deicide") and hurled incessant polemics against Jewish faith and, indeed, against God's Word in the Hebrew Scriptures (the "old Law") itself. One can see this explicit intention to break with the denigrations of the past in the strong statements and fresh phrasings the *Catechism* uses throughout the text. These provide the frame for understanding its approach.

1. The church's understanding of God's people, the Jews, is stated in the present tense, not the past tense. "Israel is the priestly people of God, 'called by the name of the Lord' (Deut 28:10) and 'the first to hear the word of God,' the people of 'elder brethren' in the faith of Abraham" (63).

2. Whatever the historical involvement of individuals, Jews as such are not collectively responsible for Jesus' death (597). The *Catechism*'s insistence on this principle and its numerous implications for classroom presentation of the New Testament is driven home by its extensive treatment under article 4 of the Creed, "suffered under Pontius Pilate, was crucified . . ." (571–630). It is under this overarching rubric rejecting the very essence of the old teaching of contempt that the *Catechism* organizes its major discussion of Jesus' relationship to the faith of his people (Israel, Law and Temple: 574–586), to which we shall return below.

3. God's Covenant with the Jewish People is "irrevocable" (839–840; 2173). The New Covenant has neither abrogated nor superseded "the First Covenant" (522). The *Catechism* is quite explicit: "The Old Covenant has never been revoked" (121). This is a reference to Pope John Paul II's framing of the issue in his extraordinary address to the Jewish community of Mainz, Germany, where he boldly likened the contemporary dialogue between the church and the Jewish people to the relationship between the Sacred Scriptures themselves: "The first dimension of this dialogue, that is, the meeting with the people of God of the Old Covenant, never revoked by God (Rom 11:29), is at the same time a dialogue within our church, that is to say, between the first and second parts of her Bible" (November 17, 1980).

4. The Hebrew Scriptures are to be presented "as the true Word of God" with their own permanent integrity and dignity. As the *Catechism* states, "the Church has always vigorously opposed the idea of rejecting the Old Testament under the pretext that the New Testament has rendered it void (Marcionism)" (123). Thus there should be an emphasis on "the unity of the divine plan" (140). As the 1974 "Vatican Guidelines for Implementing *Nostra Aetate*" fleshed out this principle: The Hebrew Bible and the Jewish tradition founded on it must not be set against the New Testament in such a way that the former seems to constitute a religion of only retributive justice, fear, and legalism, with no appeal to love of God and neighbor (Deut 6:5; Lev 19:18; Hos 11; Matt 22).

5. While Christians validly see in the Hebrew Scriptures "prefigurations of what God accomplished in the fullness of time in the person of his incarnate Son" (128), typology and fulfillment are not the only valid approaches to interpreting the Hebrew Bible. "Such typological reading discloses the inexhaustable content of the Old Testament, but it must not

make us forget that the Old Testament retains its own intrinsic value as revelation reaffirmed by Our Lord Himself" (129). This paragraph of the *Catechism* reflects Section I of the Holy See's 1985 *Notes on the Correct Way to Present Jews and Judaism in Catholic Preaching and Catechesis,* which deals at length with "the relations between the Testaments." The *Notes* urge catechists to "profit discerningly from the traditions of Jewish reading" of the Bible from ancient to modern times. This task of drawing the fruits of dialogue with Jews into the classroom has, even in our own country, only just begun. Likewise, the *Catechism* follows tradition in distinguishing the various "senses" of Scripture: "literal" (governed by critical exegesis) and "spiritual" (allegorical, moral, and analogical), with the last three "based on" the former (115–119).

6. The *Catechism* in two paragraphs (839–840) distills what it considers essential to an understanding of "the relationship of the Church with the Jewish People." The first echoes the Second Vatican Council's *Nostra aetate,* the Pope's 1986 address at the Rome Synagogue, and the prayer "for the Jewish people" from the reformed Good Friday liturgy of the Roman Missal: "When she delves into her own mystery, the Church, the People of God in the New Covenant, discovers her link with the Jewish People, 'the first to hear the Word of God.' The Jewish Faith, unlike other non-Christian religions, is already a response to God's revelation in the Old Covenant," citing then Romans 9:4-5 and 11:29, as did the Council. One will note here the distinctive intimacy of what the Council called the church's ongoing "spiritual bond" with Jews and Judaism and why the Pope called the Jews our "elder brothers" in the faith in the present tense and not as a past event exhausted in New Testament times (see also 63). The validity not only of the "first covenant" but of present-day Jewish belief and practice as a faithful "response to God's revelation" is affirmed.

7. Catechists need to look beyond past and present in speaking of "fulfillment" and imbue their teaching with eschatological urgency. "When one considers the future, God's People of the Old Covenant and the new People of God tend toward similar goals: expectation of the coming (or the return) of the Messiah." Acknowledging frankly the very real differences in messianic beliefs between Jews and Christians (and, one might add, among both Jews and Christians), this framing allows the fulfillment theology of the *Catechism* to be freeing and challenging rather than exclusivist or supersessionist. As the section of the 1985 *Notes*

of the Holy See, on which the *Catechism* here relies, states: "Attentive to the same God who has spoken, hanging on the same word, we Jews and Christians have to witness to one same memory and one common hope in God who is the master of history. We must accept our responsibility to prepare the world for the coming of the Messiah by working together for social justice . . . and international reconciliation. To this we are driven, Jews and Christians, by the command to love our neighbor, by a common hope for God's Reign, and by the great heritage of the Prophets." These sentiments of the Holy See's Commission, in turn, echo numerous similar statements of the Pope over the years.

8. Reiterating the words of Pope John Paul II to representatives of Bishops' Conferences in Rome (March 6, 1982) and the emphasis in the 1985 Vatican *Notes* that followed from the Pope's words, the *Catechism* declares that "a better knowledge of the Jewish people's faith and religious life as professed and lived even now can help our better understanding of certain aspects of Christian liturgy" (1096). This section goes on to spell out the Jewish roots of Christian liturgical practices such as the proclamation of Sacred Scripture, response of praise and intercession for the living and dead, the structure and lectionary cycle of the Liturgy of the Word and of the Hours, central prayers such as the Lord's Prayer, the great feasts of the church, and the liturgical cycle itself, especially the Passover, which "both celebrate." "For Jews it is the Passover of history, tending toward the future; for Christians it is the Passover fulfilled in the death and Resurrection of Christ, though always in expectation of its definite consummation." Again, the eschatological caveat ("already here/not yet here") calls Jews and Christians into a dialogue of mutual reconciliation, expectation, and working together to prepare the world for God's reign, a task Jews call *Tikkun Olam* (repairing the world). Again, if religious educators are to tap the spiritual richness of Jewish liturgical tradition as a resource for deepening understanding not only of Jesus but of subsequent Christian liturgical development, solid studies of Jewish sources and practices over the centuries will need to be undertaken in Catholic schools at all levels.

2. James L. Heft

I am a Catholic theologian, for the last seven years provost of a Catholic university, and I have been very interested in the Jewish-Catholic dialogue for the past two decades. I have been personally involved in this dialogue and have published a few articles about it. My purpose is twofold: first, to reflect on the German Bishops' statement, and second, to do so as someone who is an American.

Before I do either of these things, allow me to make some general comments about the publication of the *Catechism* in the United States and its reception here. As many may know, the *Catechism* was written originally in French and approved by the Pope in June of 1992, and then was quickly translated into Italian and Spanish. After a good deal of controversy, mainly over inclusive language, a problem particular to English-speaking countries, and then especially among university people, the approved English version was released in the fall of 1994.

Comments published by theologians in the United States on earlier drafts of the *Catechism* were frequently negative. An entire issue (March 3, 1990) of the Jesuit weekly, *America,* contained essays by five theologians and a bishop. At least two book-length collections of essays on the *Catechism* were also published.

Once the approved version appeared, there was widespread criticism in the press about the lack of inclusive language. Eventually, however, more positive and substantive evaluations began to appear. Thousands of copies of the *Catechism* were sold. Universities held symposia on it and dioceses throughout the country organized programs for their religion teachers to learn about its contents. Some on the Left remained critical; some on the Right wanted it used as a textbook for teaching high school and college students. Most, however, have come to see it as it was intended to be seen: as a compendium, a point of reference for official Catholic teaching.

I am impressed with the thoughtful and nuanced statement of the German discussion group on how Jews and Judaism are treated in the *Catechism.* The literature on this subject in the United States covers nearly all the same points, but not as succinctly. Typically, the positive points of the *Catechism*'s treatment are noted by us as well: the *Catechism* does not back away from the statements of Vatican II, clearly speaks of the irrevocable nature of the covenant between God and the Jews, speaks positively of Jesus' identity as a Jew and of the Pharisees, and flatly rejects the notion of any collective responsibility of the Jews for the death of Jesus. Moreover, the general consensus, if I can speak of such, is that the *Catechism* tries to include, besides the teachings of Vatican II on the Jews, the 1974 and 1985 documents of the Vatican's Commission for Religious Relations with the Jews, without, however, going beyond them, and without trying to resolve some of the difficulties that remain. Dr. Eugene Fisher, the Director of Catholic-Jewish Relations for the U.S. National Conference of Catholic Bishops, has published several articles that summarize the "centrist" reception of the *Catechism*'s teaching on the Jews.

*

The German statement points out many of the weaknesses of the *Catechism*'s treatment of the Jews, including especially the way in which "typology" can leave one with the impression that Israel should cease to exist now that the "new Israel," the church, has arrived. We speak of this in English as the theory of "supersessionism"; that is, any teaching that would suggest that Judaism has no legitimate reason to continue to exist once Jesus has appeared. The critics of the *Catechism* see supersessionism implied in such statements as "the New Testament fulfills the Old Testament" and "the Church replaces the Jews as God's people."

Without question, there is a negative interpretative side to the "typological" approach to Scripture. The Fathers of the early church frequently employed such typology, and in fact, historically, such usage fueled the flames of the "teaching of contempt," which erupted in various fatal fires for Jews throughout the history of Christianity, culminating in the massive conflagration of the *Shoah*. The roots of such supersessionism can be traced back even further, as the German Bishops observe when referring to "ecclesiastical anti-Judaism," to the very statements of the New Testament about "the Jews," especially in the Gospel of John.

The situation created by such use of typology would be partially corrected by focusing on the things Christians and Jews still hold in common: the belief in one God, a God who is merciful and compassionate, a God who forgives his people. Moreover, a positive portrait of contemporary Judaism, one that recognizes that Judaism continues to be a living religious tradition, would also help blunt the negative potential of typology. Finally, a thoughtful statement of why the church continues to have a special relationship with Judaism, one without which it could not understand itself, would make it clearer that Judaism has not been and should not be superseded.

Two final comments occur to me as I read the German statement. Both refer to the very last of three deficiencies that remain in the new *Catechism.* I agree that the *Catechism* could have made a very positive impact by pointing out that Jews and Christians, especially today and especially in the West, face a common challenge both within their own affluent communities and in confronting a world of unbelief. It was put in a striking manner by the Chief Rabbi of England, Jonathan Sacks. Speaking in London in September 1995, on the first night of *Selichot,* the penitential period that precedes the Jewish New Year, Dr. Sacks argued that the return to the land brought about by Zionism has been followed by a crisis of belief: "A hundred years ago we had the faith but not the land. Today we have the land, but what has happened to the faith?" He continued: "We understand why, in fifteenth-century Spain or in nineteenth-century Germany and Russia, Jews left the community. They were in fear for their lives. Today Jews are free and accepted and successful and above all we have a home. Is it possible that the greatest danger to Jewish survival will turn out to be, God forbid, not Nazi Germany or Soviet Russia, but our own indifference?" Dr. Sacks went on to deplore "the loss of Jewish meaning in our lives" and the "split developing between the religious minority and the secular majority, each growing yearly more extreme." The answer, he said, was for the entire Jewish people "to come to God" (*The Tablet,* 23 September 1995).

The same could be said of most Catholics in the West. Never before in history have so many Catholics been so affluent, and never before has the danger of a loss of genuine faith been greater. In view of this, Catholics and Jews face a deep common problem: genuine faith in the face of a world that is, in large part, indifferent to matters of religious faith. The *Catechism* could have made such an observation. Had it done so, both Catholics and Jews would be seen to face a similar challenge.

The second observation has to do with the difficulty of speaking about "guilt, pain, and reconciliation." The Jewish-Christian dialogue in the United States deals less with that existential *angst* rooted in the German Christian soul, especially in the last six decades. Here the discussion is often dominated on the Catholic side by various theological issues, and on the Jewish side by various political and religious issues. While our responses to the *Catechism*'s treatment of the Jews have been quite similar, the existential relationship between Jews and Christians in the United States remains less marked by the events of the last sixty years. In fact, in the late 1920s in the United States, when the campaign of the Catholic Al Smith for the presidency of our country met with strong anti-Catholicism, Catholics and Jews came together to form an organization to fight racial and religious prejudice: the National Conference of Christians and Jews, now called The National Conference. This organization remains a vital witness and force throughout the country.

*

Another thoughtful participant in the Jewish-Catholic dialogue is Fr. John Pawlikowski, a professor of Social Ethics at the Catholic Theological Union in Chicago. He recently wrote about three phases the Jewish-Catholic dialogue has gone through in the United States. The first he describes as the "cleansing" phase. Based on the teachings about the Jews at Vatican II, this phase examined educational texts used in the Catholic Church and removed from them those themes that were clearly "supersessionist." The second phase, which in some ways reaches back before Vatican II, has to do with the way in which Christian scholars are recognizing the value of the Hebrew Scriptures (the "Old Testament") in ways that allow it to stand on its own right. This movement among scholars has allowed Christians to appreciate as never before the Jewishness of Jesus and the Judaism of the time of Jesus. The third phase, continues Pawlikowski, is only now beginning. It is the effort to rethink the relationship of the church to the Jews in fundamentally new ways. Progress in this third phase will help us, I assume, to find ways to make use of "typology" without running the risk of "supersessionism," as Christians recognize Jesus as the "fulfillment" of the utterances of the Hebrew prophets without at the same time suggesting that as a consequence these prophecies no longer have a unique role for the Jewish people, and to profess Jesus as the "Savior of the world" and still affirm a continuing validity and necessity for the existence of the great living tradition of Judaism.

3. Alan Mittleman

The intervention of the dialogue group "Jews and Christians" accurately analyzes the failure of the 1992 *Catechism* to develop a coherent, positive approach to Judaism and the Jewish people. The Jewish reader of the *Catechism* cannot fail to note its conflicting tendencies. It clearly wants to continue, as the relevant predecessor documents did, what one might call a moral affirmation of Jews and Judaism. That is to say, the *Catechism* wants to eschew anti-Semitism, undo prejudice, nurture an appreciation of the richness of Judaism and of its relatedness to the church. It wants Catholics to recognize Jews as persons of faith. On the other hand, the *Catechism* falls short of generating a theology that really sustains these sorts of moral affirmation. Its moral and theological impulses are in discord.

In this regard the *Catechism* is a slightly less generous version of the 1985 *Guidelines.* Many Jewish critics of that document, including this writer, noted at the time that the reliance of the *Guidelines* on a typological hermeneutic undercuts a credible affirmation of Judaism and supports supersessionism, qualified and nuanced though it might be. If the inherent, divinely intended trajectory of the Hebrew Bible is the New Testament, as both the *Guidelines* and the *Catechism* (e.g., 140) teach, then rabbinic interpretation of Torah—the very heart of Judaism!—is necessarily off the mark. At this point the moralistic intention of the document to restore a prejudice-free reputation to the Pharisees is subverted by a theology that consigns their Judaism to the realm of illusion and confusion.

The Catholic scholar Hans Hermann Henrix, writing on the 1985 *Hinweise,* remarked that they contain a *"christologische Dialektik von Ja und Nein zu Israel"* (christological dialectics between Yes and No to Israel). Henrix takes the incoherence I have pointed to and elevates it to an interpretative principle; that is, the church's response to Israel must necessarily be dialectical. On the most optimistic reading, *"so wird man vielleicht doch von einem Ja sprechen können, welches das Nein umgreift; es ist ein Ja nicht ohne das Nein, aber das Nein bleibt im Ja integriert"* (thus one can speak of a Yes that encompasses the No; it is not a Yes without the No, but the No remains an integral part of the Yes). These remarks seem to me entirely germane to the *Catechism* as well.

But if it is true that incoherence, dialectic, and ambivalence are structural rather than contingent features of the church's theology, then on what basis do the authors of the Interjection criticize the *Catechism*? Even if it can go further on certain key points, how far can it ultimately go? Can (should) the church see the Jews as the Jews want to see themselves? Is that the ideal that theology should posit? Or must the church hold on to its dialectic of "yes" and "no" to Israel in order to remain church? These are the hard questions that *Netzakh Yisrael,* the eternity of Israel, poses, but that the *Catechism* only dimly grasps.

4. Michael A. Signer

It is with some hesitation that, as a Jew, I write (at the invitation of Professor Hanspeter Heinz) about the Central Committee's reflection on the presentation of Judaism in the new *Catechism.* The *Catechism* is a Catholic document for Catholics. According to the preface written by Pope John Paul II, the *Catechism* is to serve as the foundation for all local churches in their catechesis. How can a Rabbi offer critical comment on a document promoted by such high authority?

An initial response would be that the new *Catechism* seems to have evoked intense discussion and argument among Catholics both during its composition and after its publication. Many publications have appeared in America that comment on the *Catechism.* They have offered serious analysis of its method and its content. One might, in fact, offer the positive argument that the new *Catechism* has stirred up a very serious discussion about the most central ideas in Catholicism and will ultimately lead to a new flowering of theological literature. One American scholar indicated that the new *Catechism* will encourage the laity to become more "literate" or "learned" in their faith. As a Jew, I am encouraged by any document that promotes serious discussion about religious ideas that will encourage people to take them into their own lives.

It also seems to me that the Central Committee's analysis of the treatment of Judaism and the Jewish people within the new *Catechism* furthers the Jewish-Catholic dialogue, which has entered into an entirely new period since Vatican II's schema *Nostra aetate.* This new period, now only thirty years old, permits Jews and Catholics to speak as partners who share a family relationship—something that could not be imagined prior to 1965. It has been a source of considerable pain to me that these most fruitful discussions have occurred long after the creative interchange in

Germany between Protestant Christianity and Judaism. How would Rabbi Leo Baeck, Franz Rosenzweig, or Martin Buber have responded to the post-*Shoah* changes in the Catholic Church? From reading their literary inheritance, I would think that they would very much endorse the report of the Central Committee of German Catholics. I know that my beloved teacher, Rabbi Jakob Petuchowski, would feel that his years teaching in Germany and his intense contacts with German Catholic theologians had been well spent.

The Central Committee acknowledges that the *Catechism* maintains the most significant theological development of Vatican II: Jews are not guilty for all time of the death of Christ. Paragraph 597, both in its rubric and its explication, makes this point with great emphasis. Equally important from a Jewish perspective is paragraph 598, which makes the constructive theological claim that Christians by their own sins contribute to the death of Christ. This paragraph is important because it leaves no ambiguity about the significance of sin in Christ's crucifixion and removes Judaism and the Jewish people entirely from the theology of the Cross.

Another positive development in the *Catechism* is the presentation of the life of Jesus within the context of Judaism (574–576). The *Catechism* emphasizes the uniqueness of Jesus within the Judaism of his time. This leads to an interesting dialectical tension of positive and negative evaluation of Judaism at the time of Jesus: Paragraphs 577–582 indicate a negative perspective on Jewish Law at the time of Jesus, and at the same time Paragraphs 583–586 reveal a positive evaluation of the Jerusalem Temple.

One would certainly expect the church to present the uniqueness of Jesus with regard to other religious groups of his lifetime. However, it is somewhat surprising in light of the very sophisticated writings of Jewish and Christian biblical scholars to have Torah and Jewish observance of Torah presented in such a negative light. This will make it more difficult for Christians to come to understand Judaism as "the way of Torah." Rabbi Leon Klenicki has drawn particular attention to the use of the term "Law" in the *Catechism,* which he stresses should have been understood according to the Hebrew term *Halakha,* which means "pathway to God."

The spirit of Vatican II's message about Judaism may also be found in Paragraph 839, which repeats the initial sentence of *Nostra aetate* 4. The next sentence is original to the *Catechism* and strengthens the positive evaluation of Judaism among non-Christian religions: "The Jewish faith, unlike other non-Christian religions, is already a response to God's revelation in the Old Covenant." Judaism, as Pope John Paul II has emphasized in many speeches, occupies a unique place among non-Christian religions: it is part of the covenanted community with God. The *Catechism* concludes paragraph 839 with two citations from Romans (9:4-5; 11:29) that emphasize the unique position of Judaism.

These positive statements are seriously subverted by paragraph 840, which adds an eschatological dimension to the previous paragraph:

> And when one considers the future, God's People of the Old Covenant and the new People of God tend toward similar goals: expectation of the coming (or the return) of the Messiah. But one awaits the return of the Messiah who died and rose from the dead and is recognized as Lord and Son of God; the other awaits the coming of a Messiah whose features remain hidden till the end of time; and the latter waiting is accompanied by the drama of not knowing or of misunderstanding Jesus Christ.

Two elements in this paragraph require careful attention because they place Judaism in a pre-Vatican II position. First is the term "God's People of the Old Covenant" to describe Jews, and "new People of God" to describe Christians. Some theologians would claim that "God's People of the Old Covenant" is a positive expression of the church's esteem for the Old Covenant, which has never been revoked. However, when this expression is placed in the context of "the new People of God" it acquires a more negative tone, as if the "new" supersedes the "old." The second disturbing part of this paragraph is the final phrase, which describes the Jewish people in its eschatological expectation of the Messiah. As a Jew, I think that the *Catechism* correctly describes the classical Jewish expectation of the Messiah: "his features remain hidden until the end of time." However, the last phrase describing Jewish waiting for the eschaton as "accompanied by the drama of not knowing or of misunderstanding Jesus Christ" sounds quite offensive. The positive evaluation of Judaism is betrayed by describing Jews as they currently live in the world as less than complete. How different is this from the medieval understanding of the Jews as *perfidi,* which means "incomplete"? The statement by the Central Committee also emphasizes the oscillating and contradictory theology of the eschaton in the *Catechism* when it calls attention to paragraph 762, which gives the impression that the covenant with Israel was actually broken and replaced by the church, or that the Jews bear the responsibility for the beginning and the delay of eschatological time in paragraph 674.

It is this sense of disappointment that is captured so eloquently by the Central Committee's evaluation of the *Catechism* as "falling beneath expectations that must be put forward nowadays." I strongly support the critical comments by the Central Committee that a positive presentation of Judaism is missing in the *Catechism*. There is no attempt to reveal the beliefs about God that are common to Judaism and Christianity. One searches throughout the *Catechism* in vain to find some positive reference to the post-biblical Judaism of the Rabbis, which is truly the religion of Jews since the time of the origin of the church. Father Gerard Sloyan, an American biblical scholar, has argued that "the Christian community in effect declares the Jews a non-people by attending to them anciently but not modernly." It would seem that the authors of the *Catechism* failed to take into account the many positive statements by the Popes from John XXIII to John Paul II, as well as the statements written by the Vatican Commission on Relations with the Jews—especially the 1985 *Notes on the Correct Way to Present Jews and Judaism in Preaching and Catechesis in the Roman Catholic Church*. Theologians like Eugene Fisher and Sr. Mary Boys have noted the *Catechism*'s failure to mention the 1985 *Notes*. Professor Boys points out the irony that "an earlier ecclesial document (the 1985 *Notes*) might be read as questioning the *Catechism*." I find it curious that the *Catechism* does not mention any of the positive statements made about Judaism by local synods of bishops in the United States, Europe, or Latin America. How sad that thirty years of productive collaboration between Christians and Jews have exercised so little influence on the *Catechism*!

The Central Committee's evaluation emphasizes another significant criticism of the *Catechism:* the treatment of the relationship between the two Testaments in the Christian Bible. While the value of the Old Testament is confirmed (pars. 121–123), it is described as "perfected" only by the New Testament. This is the hermeneutical process of the entire *Catechism,* as we learn from paragraph 1963: "According to the Christian tradition the law is holy, spiritual, and from God, yet imperfect." An alternative formulation of the same idea is paragraph 1967: "The law of the Gospel fulfills, completes, surpasses, and perfects the old law." Ultimately the Law is a "pedagogue" to lead people toward Christ (par. 708). This statement is, of course, based on Galatians 3:24, but it would be difficult to teach Christians or to convince Jews that the Catholic Church holds Judaism in high esteem when the foundations of Jewish revelation are described as less than complete. While this may have been a perfectly reasonable historical description of the ways Christians have understood the Law as part of God's revelation, I wonder why it remains necessary for the *Catechism* to maintain such a strong apologetic and defensive tone.

From the critique of the relationship between the two testaments of the Christian Bible arise serious questions by the Central Committee and American theologians about the use of typology as a teaching device in the *Catechism*. Many Jewish theologians became concerned about typological interpretation after the 1985 *Notes* appeared. Christian theologians also expressed some doubts about the *Notes'* presentation of typologies. The *Catechism* would confirm their initial impressions.

If the Old Testament is "imperfect," then it serves only as a shadow of the reality established in the New Testament. This typological formula appears in the Epistle to the Hebrews and in apostolic writings such as the *Letter of Barnabas*, the *Didache*, and the *Apostolic Constitutions*. The darker side of typological interpretation in the early church is revealed in Melito of Sardis' *Homily on Passover*. The positive statements about Judaism in the *Catechism* provide a defense against a negative image of the Old Testament. However, uncritical readers of the *Catechism* are most likely to quickly pass over the lessons of the Hebrew Bible to move on to the church. The danger of Marcionism is, therefore, always present in reading those portions of the *Catechism* that focus on the sacraments and life of the church.

How unfortunate that readers of the *Catechism* will not approach typology with the more sophisticated ideas expressed in the Pontifical Biblical Commission's statement of 1994:

> The Church reads the Old Testament in light of the Paschal Mystery, the death and resurrection of Jesus Christ, who brings a radical newness and sovereign authority, and gives a meaning to Scripture that is decisive and definitive (cf. *Dei verbum* 4). This new determination of meaning has become an integral element of the Christian faith. It ought not, however, mean doing away with all attempts to be consistent with that earlier canonical interpretation which preceded the Christian Passover. One must respect each stage of the history of salvation. To empty the Old

> Testament of its own prophetic meaning would be to deprive the New Testament of its roots in history.

As a Jew it would never be my expectation that Christians would not emphasize their own reading of the Hebrew Bible in light of the kerygma of their faith. However, as the Pontifical Biblical Commission has stated, "One must respect each stage of the history of salvation." When the *Catechism* uses simple correspondences between events in the Christian Bible as its typological foundation, it empties the Christian tradition of part of its rich heritage. As Mary Boys has argued: "The *Catechism* uses typology that is a liturgical and poetic method and transforms it into prose and proposition." When poetry is turned into prose it loses its power to transform the human spirit.

When I think about the new *Catechism,* I trust that it will be well interpreted by my Catholic colleagues in Europe, North America, and Latin America who have worked so intensively in the dialogue. They have sought out Jews who have helped them to a better understanding of Judaism, of the Jews as a people living God's word in the world. My concern is for those Catholics whose sole guide to Judaism will be the *Catechism.* In the remote corners of Africa and Asia where there are many Catholics who will never meet a living Jew, how will their attitudes toward Judaism develop? Will they learn from Catholics who have experienced Judaism? Or will they simply read the *Catechism,* with all the tensions and contradictions the report of the Central Committee has uncovered?

My hope is that the church of Africa and Asia will learn from the experiences of those who have participated together with Jews in dialogue. I pray that those Catholics who have learned about Jews and Judaism from the actions and speeches of the Pope, the synods of bishops, and the writings of theologians will transmit those teachings *verbo et exemplo.* If the church of the Third Millennium is not to repeat the sins of the Second Millennium, the world depends on them.

Reflections on the *Shoah*: The Catholic Church's Share of the Blame and Responsibility

September 4, 1998

On March 16, 1998, the Vatican Commission for Religious Relations with the Jews published the document *We Remember: A Reflection on the* Shoah, which had been in preparation for ten years. On September 1, 1987, Pope John Paul II had already emphasized that the planned publication was "important for the Church and the World" and that the *Shoah* was "a warning, a testimony, and a mute outcry for the whole human race."[1]

The declaration has had a remarkable resonance throughout the world. There was both approval and criticism. The discussion group "Jews and Christians" of the Central Committee of German Catholics, which consists of eleven Jewish and seventeen Catholic members, has analyzed the declaration and is presenting its position here. While recognizing the significance of the document, the group would like to make some suggestions in view of the papal message scheduled for the year 2000, the "Year of Reconciliation."

We gratefully acknowledge that the Roman declaration is a further step on the path to establishing a new relationship with Judaism. The Second Vatican Council's declaration *Nostra aetate* was the first step on this path, and since then many pronouncements and initiatives of the Catholic Church have continued this work. Important insights garnered from this process can be found again in the document "We Remember."

1. Quoted from the *Freiburger Rundbrief*, new ed., March 1998, p. 161.

It refers emphatically to the Jewish roots of the Christian faith. It gives historical examples of the guilt of Christians with respect to Jews. In agreement with the way Jews see themselves, it recognizes "the unique witness of the Jewish people to the Holy One of Israel and to the Torah." For the first time ever a Vatican document uses the term *Shoah,* i.e., annihilation or calamity (cf., e.g., Isa 10:3), which excludes any religious interpretation whatsoever such as the one suggested, for example, by the term "Holocaust," i.e., burnt offering (cf. e.g., Gen 22:2). The document contains repeated and urgent insistence on the Christian duty to remember the *Shoah.*

In spite of such remarkable statements, the document's historical and theological propositions unfortunately fall short of earlier declarations by Pope John Paul II, the National Conference of German Bishops, and several French Bishops.[2] More than anything else we miss a forthright statement concerning the church's share of blame and responsibility. It is not enough simply to mention the "errors and failures of . . . sons and daughters of the church." Following the lead of the Council, the German bishops rightly emphasized in 1988, on the occasion of the fiftieth anniversary of *Reichskristallnacht* ("The Night of Broken Glass"), "that the church, which we profess to be holy and revere as a mystery, is also a sinful church in need of repentance."[3]

1. Slow Disassociation of the Church from Judaism

The Vatican document gives the impression that the process in which the "early church" and the "Jewish People" split apart already began immediately "after the crucifixion of Jesus." We consider this to be historically inaccurate. The long process during which the church disassociated itself from the Jewish people must be seen in a more differentiated way.

A Vatican declaration from the year 1985 states: "Jesus was and always remained a Jew . . . Jesus was fully a man of his time and of his environment: the Jewish-Palestinian one of the first century, the anxieties and hopes of which he shared. . . . Paul also, like Jesus himself, used methods

2. Cf. Pope John Paul II, "Speech at the Synagogue of Rome," April 13, 1986; "Accepting the Burden of History," message of the Berlin, German, and Austrian Conferences of Bishops, October 20, 1988; declaration of several French bishops in Drancy, 1997.

3. "Accepting the Burden of History," no. 2; cf. Vatican Council II, *Lumen Gentium,* § 8.

of reading and interpreting Scripture and of teaching his disciples which were common to the Pharisees of their time."[4] The controversial discussions found in the books of the New Testament are initially inner-Jewish disputes.

Seeing Jewish hopes reconfirmed and fulfilled in Jesus as the Christ, New Testament communities gradually began to disassociate themselves from Judaism. When the Greek-speaking communities reverted to the Greek translation of the Hebrew Bible (the Septuagint), the process was accelerated, not least through the assimilation of Greek ideas. The inclusion of the New Testament books in the canon of biblical books is an expression of a particular identity and witnesses to the belief in God's acting through Jesus of Nazareth.

The Christianity that finally took shape entered increasingly into rivalry with Judaism. "In the Christian world . . . erroneous and unjust interpretations of the New Testament regarding the Jewish people and their alleged culpability . . . circulated," and these even led to the destruction of some synagogues. This assertion of the Roman document is indeed accurate, but not adequate as regards the first centuries.

Gentile-Christian theologians (apologists and church fathers) reinforced the church practice of viewing the New Testament texts exclusively with Gentile-Christian eyes and changing the condemnation of some Jews into a condemnation of the Jewish people. What originally started out as a "family conflict" within Judaism developed more and more into a theologically supported enmity toward another religion.[5] As a rule the Patristic authors, whose writings would become important for subsequent history, laid claim to the salvation history of the Old Testament as a prehistory of the church and denied the Jewish people their right to biblical election and promise (substitution theory, disinheritance theory).

This development was further intensified when Christianity became the state religion of the Roman empire. The political theology at the time of Constantine (Eusebius) regarded this historic turning point as subsequent proof of the messianic status of Jesus Christ. The Jews, on the other hand, had to resign themselves to becoming an insignificant minority in

4. *Notes on the Correct Way to Present the Jews and Judaism in Preaching and Catechesis in the Roman Catholic Church,* declaration of the Vatican Commission for Religious Relations with the Jews, 24 June 1985, nos. 12 and 18.

5. Cf. the "Adversus Judaeos" literature of the church fathers.

the Christian empire. In the period that followed, the church emphasized its superiority more and more and forgot the root—Israel—from which it permanently stems.

Only with the Second Vatican Council was a redefinition of the relationship with the Jewish people inaugurated. Referring to Paul's letter to the Romans, the declaration *Nostra aetate* urgently calls on Christians to stop denying Jews their religious right to exist and leaves it up to the hidden will of God how the salvation of "all Israel" will take place (cf. Rom 9:11). Is the humility of not knowing why the dramatic separation between Christianity and Judaism occurred not part of the respect owed to the mystery of God? It should be recognized, as Joseph Cardinal Ratzinger said, that "Overcoming this separation is not within our power. Rather, the separation keeps us together on the path toward what will be, and therefore there must be no enmity between us."[6]

This brief overview shows that only the most precise possible study of the gradual process of separation will enable us to set a different course in the relationship between Jews and Christians as drawn from the experience of our own century. We therefore call upon everyone who today studies the history of the first centuries to discover and present the connections between Jews and Christians and thus to do the work of reconciliation.

2. *Problematic Decisions by Ecumenical Councils as Statements of the Whole Church*

With respect to the church's self-evaluation in relation to Judaism, the Vatican text seems to us to be unconvincing when it assigns blame to individual Christians yet excludes from blame the church itself as a constituted faith community. This was not true even of the medieval church, and it is just as invalid for the first half of the twentieth century.

The significance of the ecumenical councils for the formation of Christian understanding of the faith is undisputed. They are official statements of the church, particularly when they are not developing a new body of thought but defining in a binding way an awareness that is already present in the church. In the Middle Ages intersecting historical, ecclesiastical-political, and economic relationships gave rise to an anti-Jewish sentiment

6. Joseph Cardinal Ratzinger, *Many Religions—One Covenant: Israel, the Church and the World* (San Francisco: Ignatius Press, 1999) 106.

that continued to be influential far into the modern age. The Vatican declaration says that "there have been centuries-old sentiments of mistrust and hostility that we call anti-Judaism."

Not only individual Christians have been guilty, however, but also ecumenical councils, in particular the Fourth Lateran Council (1215), which was to enjoy special standing in the West. This council made a general accusation that the Jews are guilty of faithlessness *(perfidia)*. Regulations that, for the most part, had long since been in effect were made binding. These pertained to Jews' money-lending businesses, the requirement that they wear identifying marks or garments, the limitation of movement and curfews, and a ban on holding public office. Above all, strict regulations were promulgated for baptized Jews.[7] In 1434 the Council of Basel endorsed a text that was no less explicit. Since this was an assembly that was exceptionally consensus-oriented and took all minority votes into consideration, it is surprising that the Decree on the Jews apparently passed without a struggle. This is further proof of a widespread anti-Jewish attitude in the church. The Basel Decree on the Jews concluded with the directive that it should be proclaimed "at least once a year at Mass in the individual cathedrals and collegiate churches and in other religious establishments in which the faithful assemble in large numbers."[8] Finally, in the Bull of Union with the Coptic Church, dated February 4, 1442, the Council of Florence applied the phrase "outside the church there is no salvation" to the Jews as well.[9] In this situation the decrees issued repeatedly by the popes for the protection of the Jews *("Sicut Judaeis")* could prevent neither pogroms nor accusations that Jews were guilty of supposed ritual murders, poisoning wells, and desecrating hosts.

Finally, we should note that in contrast to the practice of all the other Western European countries the Papal States, which had been established anew after the Napoleonic Wars, readopted a discriminatory policy toward the Jews by establishing ghettos and requiring Jews to wear identifying marks or garments. Once again the Jews were strictly forbidden to employ Christian servants; "compulsory sermons" were reintroduced: five times a year the Jews had to listen to sermons given for the purpose

7. Cf. *Conciliorum Oecumenicorum Decreta*, 265–67.

8. Cf. *Conciliorum Oecumenicorum Decreta*, 483–85, at 485.

9. Cf. *Conciliorum Oecumenicorum Decreta*, especially 578.

of proselytizing them. The baptism of Jewish children without parental consent, which often led to the removal of the baptized person from the family (e.g., in the Mortara Affair of 1858 in the Papal States), had a very negative effect on the relationship between the Catholic Church and Judaism.

In *Nostra aetate* the Second Vatican Council broke with the previous tradition for the first time and risked taking a new approach to Christianity's relationship with Judaism. With this development all that had gone before was *de facto* revoked.

3. The Connection Between Christian Anti-Judaism and Pagan Anti-Semitism

"The *Shoah* was the work of a thoroughly modern neo-pagan regime. Its anti-Semitism had its roots outside Christianity." We must contradict this assertion of the Vatican declaration. It is true that, compared with the anti-Judaism of the church, the anti-Semitism of the Nazi regime attained a new dimension with its racial doctrines and its determination to exterminate the Jews. But we are convinced that this pagan anti-Semitism would not have been possible if Christian anti-Judaism had not laid the foundation. This is supported by the historical indications we have cited.

The statements of the Vatican text concerning the behavior of church figures during the National Socialist period are also inadequate, even misleading. This is particularly true in the cases of Cardinal Faulhaber, Cardinal Bertram, and Pope Pius XII. In December 1933 the Archbishop of Munich, Michael Cardinal von Faulhaber, preached on the great respect Catholics have for the Old Testament. He claimed the Old Testament as belonging to Christianity, asserting that it did indeed originate within Judaism but that it was not really a Jewish book. One should therefore not transfer antipathy toward contemporary Judaism to the Old Testament, as the National Socialists and the German Christians had done by rejecting it as a "Book of the Jews." The courage of the Munich archbishop was admired because of his Advent sermons. From that point on he was regarded at home and abroad as the guarantor and spiritual leader of Catholic resistance.

He could not, of course, live up to such high expectations. It should be remembered that Faulhaber had no objection to "genuine racial research and the cultivation of one's race." His sermons were also marked by a classical anti-Judaism (rejection and flight as a divine stigma of the "eternal Jew"). Neither he nor any of his fellow German bishops protested against the boycott of the Jews on April 1, 1933, or against the Nuremberg Laws.

The clear criticism in the sermons of Bernhard Lichtenberg, dean of the cathedral of Berlin, stands in stark contrast to the silence of the German bishops. He spoke out against the forced sterilization of the chronically ill and the euthanasia-murders of the disabled. His assistance to persecuted "Non-Aryans" and his public prayer for the victims of the *Reichskristallnacht* ultimately resulted in his being harassed and arrested. After two years of punishment in prison he died while being transported to the Dachau concentration camp. His exceptional witness may not be mentioned in the same breath with that of Faulhaber or even Bertram, which is what the Vatican document does. Other men and women—we are thinking, for example, of the dauntless Gertrud Luckner from Freiburg—should have been mentioned.

The letter of the Berlin Bishop Graf von Preysing is one of the few interventions that became public after 1945. He had asked Cardinal Bertram, the Chairman of the National Conference of German Bishops, to make public at least one of his many petitions to the National Socialist government. Preysing, however, could not prevail over Bertram and the majority of the bishops.

On March 6, 1943, Preysing had turned to Pope Pius XII. The pope, however, decided "to exercise restraint in order to avert greater harm." Pius XII abided by this decision even when thousands of Jews were deported from Rome before his very eyes to be taken to Auschwitz, which he knew. Regardless of how the role of this pope as head of the whole church will be judged in the end with regard to the Jewish question, we are convinced that Pius XII, as Bishop of Rome, should have intervened publicly at least on behalf of the Jews of his city. Even if he perhaps could not have saved them from death, his action would have been a model for other bishops.

The Pope did speak out in favor of hiding Jews in monasteries and convents. Jewish emigrants thanked him for this. But after 1945 it came to light that in some of the monasteries and convents zealots had baptized Jewish children against their will. Enormous efforts were required in order to return them to their Jewish families.

After the end of the war it soon became public knowledge that church agencies, especially in Rome, had access to safe channels to neutral foreign countries. These church organizations also assisted people who were deeply involved in the criminal machinery of the National Socialists. In this way, with the help of the church, criminals also succeeded in fleeing to the Middle East and from there to Latin America.

All in all, the stance of the Catholic Church toward the *Shoah* is ambivalent, if not one to be ashamed of. The words of Pope John Paul II, with which the Vatican document begins, are accurate: that Christians, "instead of offering to the world the witness of a life inspired by the values of faith manifested ways of thinking and acting which were truly forms of counter-witness and scandal."

4. Admission of Blame and Responsibility for History

The Vatican declaration emphasizes the power of reconciliation and the duty of remembering: "The common future of Jews and Christians demands that we remember, for there is no future without memory." The duty of remembering presupposes an exact knowledge of historical facts and demands a scientific analysis of the past without any kind of apologetic. As the declaration states, many studies on the National Socialist period are yet to be undertaken: "Historians, sociologists, philosophers, politicians, psychologists and theologians are all trying to gain a deeper insight into the reality of the *Shoah* and its causes." Therefore, in our understanding, it follows that the Vatican Archives must be opened so that the relevant documents can be studied.

The relationship between Judaism and Christianity must be sustained by mutual respect and recognition, since "Jews and Christians encounter each other in a comparable hope founded on the same promise made to Abraham."[10] The integrity of our will to seek renewal requires of all members of the church that they admit that they have incurred blame and are responsible for history. We continue to hope that in the papal message already scheduled for the year 2000, the "Year of Reconciliation," the church, precisely as an institution, will recognize and confess her share of the blame and her responsibility.

10. *Notes on the Correct Way to Present the Jews and Judaism* (see n. 4), § 10; there is a reference to Gen 12:1-3 and Heb 6:13-18.

In his introductory letter Pope John Paul II expresses his hope that the declaration *We Remember: A Reflection on the* Shoah may "enable memory to play its necessary part in the process of shaping a future in which the unspeakable iniquity of the *Shoah* will never again be possible." It is the duty of all Christians at all levels of church activity to proceed along the path taken by the Second Vatican Council.

A Journey to the Holy Land

Revised edition of 1998

Preface

People have different reasons for traveling to the Holy Land. Some want to make a pilgrimage to the biblical sites to see the places closely linked with the origins of their faith. Others plan a study tour, hoping to learn more about the past and the present, religion and politics, and the country and people of Israel; many will probably try to combine these things during their trip. The primary aim of this little booklet provided by the discussion group "Jews and Christians," organized by the Central Committee of German Catholics, is to provide all travelers to the Holy Land with information regarding the religious situation in Israel, and at the same time to stimulate renewed reflection on Jewish-Christian relations.

Since 1971 Jewish and Christian members of the group have been meeting to discuss their various relationships. Several publications have resulted, reminding Jews and Christians of their common heritage and reappraising the heavy burden of history they both must bear. Members of the discussion group have also repeatedly brought to mind the joint responsibility of Jews and Christians for the present and future good of humankind, based on their belief in God and the ethics taught in the Bible. The same motivation inspired the discussion group to publish this booklet. It reveals that, in different ways for Jews and Christians, the Holy Land is not only the place of their origin, but also the scene of so many past occurrences that continue to influence their lives to this day. Because this land was also important for Muslims right from the beginning, Islam cannot be ignored.

A journey to the Holy Land can intensify age-old misunderstandings among the three great monotheistic religions. But it can also lead to better communication and understanding, providing the country is not regarded as a museum but as a place in which to encounter the people who live there now.

The present booklet is a revised edition of two previous editions with the same title, published in 1974 and 1984. These have been widely read and were well received, but the time has come to update them. Many thanks must be expressed to two members of the group, Werner Trutwin and Hermann Henrix, for writing the booklet and for helping with the revision, as well as to all the members for their useful suggestions.

Bonn, Christmas 1997
Prof. Dr. Hans Joachim Meyer
President, Central Committee of German Catholics

Expectations

The Holy Land is made up primarily of the territory of the state of Israel, the autonomous Palestinian territories, and the Sinai desert, which belongs to Egypt. It is the country venerated by three religions. Here, for three-and-a-half millennia, Judaism has received its religious, political, and cultural shaping. Abraham, Moses, and the prophets have been of vital importance right from the beginning and throughout Jewish history. The Holy Land is a living center of Jewish faith. Its religion is not linked with particular holy sites there, but with the land itself. It is the promise and gift of God to this people. Christianity springs from the Jewish heritage and links the country with the life and teachings of Jesus of Nazareth. From here the Gospel went out to the whole world. After Medina and Mecca, Jerusalem is the holiest city for Muslims. Mohammed himself was linked with this city in many ways. The three great monotheistic religions have their roots in the Holy Land and regard it as containing important sites of their origins. Since the beginning of their history it has been for Jews the "promised land." To this day the holy sites have remained the goal of Jewish, Christian, and Muslim pilgrimage. Although Judaism, Christianity, and Islam have quite different relationships to the Holy Land, those relationships are not incompatible.

Surprisingly, despite the present-day lack of interest in religious traditions, pilgrimages have remained popular—in fact, it would seem that their significance is being rediscovered. Just as in former times, today's pilgrims—especially the young people among them—hope that a visit to sacred places will strengthen their faith and give new meaning to their spiritual life. A pilgrimage links the paths of earth with a destination beyond this world. Those who set out on such a journey expect to be able to leave their routine lives behind them for a while—to get to know themselves better as they travel, to share new experiences with others, to enter into another world, and to gain a deeper understanding of the religious dimension of their lives. Exertion and rest, peace and adventure, seeing and praying, freshness and fatigue—experiencing one's own limitations—are always part of the journey. Moving from place to place, arriving, departing, and setting out anew become for the traveler an image of life itself, a symbol of human existence the pilgrim can live and feel.

Pilgrimage today is often replaced by an educational or study tour, which gives particular attention to ancient monuments, art, unusual features of the landscape, social structures, and the present political situation. Christians traveling to the Holy Land can certainly combine the aims of a pilgrimage and a study tour. One need not exclude the other. At the same time, a visitor who does not share the beliefs of the peoples of the Holy Land will understand the country better if he or she knows more about the faith that is linked with its people and places. Anyone who completely shuts out the religious dimension of the country will find it much more difficult to understand its reality.

It would, however, be wrong to assume that it is possible to come closer to God here than anywhere else. According to biblical faith God is not bound to a particular place. He can be found wherever people open their hearts to him. A person seeking God does not need to travel to the Holy Land. But the pilgrim might possibly be stimulated by experiences in the Holy Land to renew the search for God in his or her own world.

I. The Reality

1. The Land

The area known to travelers as the "Holy Land" has many names originating from manifold traditions and experiences. Each of these names has a special fascination for those who use it to describe their land.

- "Land of Israel" *(Eretz Israel)* has been used by the Jews to name this land since biblical times. It originates from the name given to the patriarch Jacob after he wrestled all night with the "angel" (Gen 32:23-31). In a widespread but controversial interpretation "Israel" is translated as "he who fights with God," which suggests that Jacob, and later also the people of Israel, were repeatedly in conflict with God. The new state, founded in 1948, adopted the name "Land of Israel," which also reminds the Jewish people of the promises God gave Abraham and the other patriarchs when he promised this land to them (Gen 15:18; 26:3; 28:13-15; Exod 6:4; Deut 6:23). It is also known as the "Promised Land," the "Land of Promise," and the "Land of Milk and Honey." It is the land to which the Israelites went when they escaped from slavery in Egypt (Exodus). And it is the country for which the Jews yearned whenever, in the course of their changing history, they lived in exile or in the Diaspora. Since, for religious Jews, God's promise is inseparably linked with *Eretz Israel*, the land is not only a geographic or political entity for them—it is, above all, a gift of God.
- "Palestine," which means "Land of the Philistines," originally referred only to the area settled by the "Philistines" on the Mediterranean coast. At the end of the second millennium B.C.E. Israel felt seriously threatened by their highly developed military power, and it was not until the reign of King David in the tenth century B.C.E. that the Israelites were able to ward off this danger. We are reminded of this period in the well-known legend of the fight between little David and the heavily armed Philistine Goliath (1 Sam 17). The name "Palestine" was given to the land later by the Romans in order to suppress the memory of Israel and the Jewish people. The name was then taken up by the fathers of the church and the crusaders as well as by the Greeks, the Arabs, and the Turks. After World War I

the English gave the name "Palestine" to the whole mandated territory. Today "Palestine" is a highly political term that is used by the Palestinians to name their national territory. The Holy Land is their home country, just as it is for Israel. It is tragic that the claims of these two peoples are in such conflict.

- The name "Holy Land" appears in the Old Testament when Moses hears a voice from the burning bush saying that the place where he is standing is "consecrated ground" or "holy land" (Exod 3:5). The same expression is used by the prophet Zechariah for Judah and Jerusalem (Zech 2:16). Christians adopted this expression later, though it is not to be found in the New Testament. In Islam the only city said to be holy is Jerusalem, which is reflected in its Arabic name, "Al Kuds" (sanctuary).

Quite contradictory concepts are linked with the term "Holy Land." In the "Holy Land" we encounter a geographic entity, accessible to everybody, and the closeness of God, whom we can only experience through faith. Thus the "Holy Land" can be both a profound religious concept and a geographical entity. The people of Israel believe that the promises made in the "Holy Land" were meant for them, but through Christianity these promises have given hope to people all over the world. The salvation once proclaimed here is still powerfully effective in the present; people hope for its final fulfillment in the future. All these things that seem so contradictory to the traveler are joined together in the Holy Land.

The nature of what is "holy" is, however, distorted in many ways in this country. Frequently current events take priority and determine life more than religion. The secularization experienced by travelers in their own countries has spread here, too, and it is often accompanied by lack of interest or appreciation for religion. In addition, the pilgrim encounters busy oriental bazaars at the holy sites, almost impossible to avoid. Persistent dealers in devotional objects and religious kitsch can sometimes detract considerably from the sacred atmosphere.

But still worse is the conflict among the religions in the Holy Land. The Israelis are continually arguing over such questions as how to keep the Sabbath, while in the Church of the Holy Sepulchre the various Christian churches find it hard to agree on their rights, and Muslims fight each other because they cannot agree on a common attitude toward Israel. The disputes among the religions can be particularly terrible at times. Clashes involving bloodshed are not a thing of the past, but still continue today. The Holy Land in particular is still confronted with senseless religious struggles, fanatical violence, and obtuse fundamentalism—clearly Jews, Christians, and Muslims do not live in the peace *(Shalom/Salaam)* their religions expect of them. We can only hope that, in the Holy Land, too, all religions will soon develop the potential for peace that is the basis for their most admirable traditions.

The traveler's encounter with the Holy Land can be moving or disappointing, pleasing or annoying, overwhelming or depressing. But if these varied experiences can help them to understand what the Holy Land is all about, they will also have experienced something of what the Talmud (which, together with the Bible, constitutes the basis of Judaism) teaches, namely: "The air of the Land of Israel makes people wise" (*Baba Bathra* 158b).

2. Jews in Israel

Israel is the land that was promised to Abraham: "I give this land to your descendants" (Gen 12:7). Every Jewish generation associates Israel with its origin and the core of its existence. Here the children of Israel found a home after their forced stay in Egypt. From the Old Testament we learn how Moses led them to Israel after their miraculous escape from the enemy on the shores of the Reed Sea after they had wandered aimlessly for years in the desert, and how at Mount Sinai they received the Ten Commandments from God.

In the Promised Land the great prophets proclaimed the Word of God, berating the people for their sins and comforting them, reminding them of God's commandments and, in hours of darkness, giving them hope for salvation. Here Israel's great teachers of wisdom lived and reflected on the mystery of God bringing the people of Israel closer to him. This is where the Psalms were written, in which Jews expressed their praise and thanksgiving to God, telling him of their suffering or even turning on him when they did not understand his ways. Here, even in biblical times, the people suffered disasters such as famine, pillage, and war.

From here, in the sixth century B.C.E., Jews were led into captivity in Babylon and held there for decades. It was to this land, too, that they could then return and set about rebuilding under difficult conditions. It was here that the Holy Scriptures of Israel were written and this is where the great rabbis developed the traditions that have remained a source of life for the Jews until today. Here and in Babylon the Talmuds were written—the great Jewish anthology in which the rabbis reflect on the teachings of God and on how, with serious regard for the irrefutable Jewish principles of loving God and loving one's neighbor, they should be interpreted in different times and situations. During the Jewish-Roman war in 70 C.E. the Temple in Jerusalem was destroyed, and in later battles the Jewish resistance against Rome was completely crushed. As a result many Jews could no longer live in their homeland. They had to go to other lands, thus enlarging the Jewish Diaspora that had existed for centuries around the Mediterranean and in Babylon.

But Jews have always lived in Israel, following the religious injunction to settle in the land of Israel and cultivate the land. Here in the Middle Ages, too, men appeared claiming to be the messiah. Rabbis and mystics kept alive the old traditions of Israel. In addition, in every century innumerable Jews came to the land as pilgrims, many with the desire to find their final resting place on the Mount of Olives. In the nineteenth century Jewish immigration increased considerably through the arrival of Chassidic communities from Eastern Europe with their mystical longing for Zion. To escape persecution, other Jewish groups came from Russia, the Balkans, and Yemen. After 1900 secular Zionist pioneers enthusiastically set about turning the eroded, marshy, and limestone landscape into fertile land. But the greatest wish expressed by Jews all over the world in their annual celebration of the Passover was and still is: "Next year in Jerusalem."

The Holy Land has always been a bridge between Europe, Asia, and Africa, and as such has been since time immemorial a place through which conquerors and their armies passed. There is still evidence today of the influence of Egyptians, Assyrians, Babylonians, Persians, Greeks, Romans, Arabs, crusaders, Mongols, Turks, and British, especially in many buildings.

At the end of the nineteenth century the age-old Jewish yearning for Jerusalem acquired political significance. Discrimination and persecution in Christian countries had gradually turned the thoughts of many Jews back to the Promised Land. Theodor Herzl (1860–1904), a Jewish journalist from Vienna and father of Zionism, brought a feeling of unity among the Jewish people, and encouraged many of them to reestablish their home in the land of their ancestors at Mount Zion in Jerusalem. Some Jews, however, disapproved of Zionism, believing that Jewish communities could survive in the Diaspora and that there they should represent the worldwide dimension of Judaism.

In 1919 the League of Nations mandated the former Turkish territory between the Mediterranean and the Iraqi desert to Great Britain as "Palestine." The land to the east of the Jordan River became an independent kingdom. The original intention in 1937 to divide Palestine into Jewish and Arabic states was prevented by disputes in the country and by World War II.

During World War II about six million Jews—among them more than one million children—were murdered by the Nazis. The *Shoah* (i.e., disaster, extermination) gave many Jews a reason to think differently about Zionism and to accept Israel as a place of refuge. Thus the greatest catastrophe in Jewish history became a historical prerequisite for the founding of a new Jewish state. On 14 May 1948, with the tacit agreement of the United Nations, the founding of the Jewish state—which was named after the biblical "Israel"—was proclaimed by David Ben Gurion, the first Prime Minister of Israel. The new state offers Jews from all over the world the opportunity of finding a home in a country where they can at last be free from domination by non-Jews. Although many secular Jews see the foundation of their state as the result of a combination of political, social, and psychological factors, the opinion of religious Jews is divided. The ultra-orthodox minority rejects the state as not being the work of the messiah, but other religious groups are able to see the rebirth of the Jewish state as the beginning of redemption and a symbol of God's love for his people.

The Jews living in Israel come from all over the world and from many cultures. The incentives for their immigration are both religious and political; some want to live in the ancient biblical Israel, others in a modern state, and many came simply to escape persecution in their homeland.

According to their country of origin, Israelis can be divided into three main groups. The Ashkenazi Israelis stem from Eastern Europe as well as Germany, France, and the United States. The Sephardic Israelis from the Mediterranean countries are descendants of the Jewish generations who were banished from Spain by the Catholic kings in 1492. Oriental Israelis mostly stem from Africa and Asia. Most of these immigrants had to learn Modern Hebrew *(Ivrith)* in the country itself, which was especially difficult for the elderly people. In recent years the arrival of many Jews from the former Soviet Union and Africa has caused severe social and economic problems, with emigration from Israel rising and falling according to the changing political and economic situation in the country.

Judaism in Israel is not unified. People have come from all over the world and are trying—in spite of their multicultural backgrounds—to create a free Jewish society in Israel. Their integration is a central task of Israeli society. The religious trends in Israel are comparable to those existing today among Jews abroad. They differ mostly in their interpretation of the religious laws, the *Halacha* (from the verb "to walk"), upon which religious Jews base their lives.

- Even today Orthodox Jews (approximately twelve percent of the Jewish population in Israel) adhere strictly to the rules of the *Halacha,* especially in Israel, where it is easier for them to live accordingly. Laws on nutrition and marriage are meticulously observed, the Sabbath is strictly kept, and tradition determines the role of Jewish women. In synagogues women sit separately from men and do not lead public worship. They do, however, pray regularly and hold religious services among themselves. Only orthodox rabbis can carry out important legal functions, for instance in family law, marriage, and divorce. They must be recognized by the Chief Rabbinate, which consists of an Ashkenazi and a Sephardic rabbi and constitutes the highest religious authority in the country. The orthodox Jews are politically active and have a number of religious parties that, although represented by few members in parliament (the Knesset), have disproportionate political influence as coalition partners. For decades politics related to religion has most frequently been the cause of government crises in Israel, splitting the country into different camps. One can hardly call religion an integrating force in Israel.
- The so-called Ultra-Orthodox Jews consider themselves the only true defenders of Jewish tradition. They refuse to recognize the state of Israel since it is not the work of the messiah, keeping strictly to the religious rules of the *Halacha* and the way of life originally developed in Eastern Europe. They determine the appearance of the district of Mea Shearim in Jerusalem, where the men wear long

black clothes, have side-locks, and in public cover their head with a hat. They will abuse or throw stones at anyone who drives a car on the Sabbath or simply strikes a match in their presence. Not only are they hostile toward the state; they also reject the authority of the Chief Rabbinate.

- The representatives of Reform Judaism (approximately nine percent) emphasize the importance of updating the structure and laws of their religion. Many laws are understood as being conditioned by a certain period in Jewish piety, but they emphasize the abiding significance of the spiritual and ethical principles of Jewish tradition. Dietary laws are no longer applied unconditionally; it is up to the individual to decide how to keep them. Women enjoy the same liturgical rights as men—in fact, since the 1980s there have been women rabbis in Reform communities—and special clothing is no longer worn.
- Between the Orthodox and Reform Jews are the Conservatives (approximately three percent), who neither want to adapt completely to present-day thinking nor adhere strictly to religious laws. Thus they try to keep the laws of the *Halacha* to the extent this is possible in today's world. At home, for example, they eat according to the dietary laws and they observe the Sabbath, but they are more lenient when traveling or when visiting non-Jewish friends. Men and women are no longer separated in the synagogue and women take on liturgical functions. Some communities have women rabbis. Marriages solemnized by conservative or reform-oriented rabbis are not recognized by the state.
- Two smaller groups have been separated from rabbinic Judaism for some time: about twelve thousand Karaites in the district of Ramallah recognize the Bible but not the rabbinic interpretation of it, and about six hundred Samaritans live in Holon and on Mount Gerizim, which has been sacred to them since biblical times and is still their only place of worship.
- The number of non-religious Israelis (approximately 75 percent), is very much larger than those who are religious (approximately 25 percent, of whom half are strictly religious and the other half less so), although it is very difficult to make a clear distinction between the religious and secular Jews; most are predominantly influenced by Western secular culture but do not reject all forms of religious

life. They oppose the strong influence the minority of Orthodox Jews exerts in public life but are unable to prevent what they see as a kind of religious coercion. Although in conflict situations they prefer laws passed in Parliament to the rabbinic *Halacha,* they keep Jewish holidays and traditions because they consider them to be part of their Jewish culture.

There is no state religion in Israel. All religious communities have the right to practice their religion freely and are entitled to government support. Christians and Muslims have their own state-recognized courts, which have jurisdiction over matters of family law such as marriage, divorce, and inheritance.

The Temple Mount in Jerusalem is a most sacred site for Jews; although under Muslim control since the Arabs captured Jerusalem in 638 and erected the Dome of the Rock and the Al-Aqsa mosque on it, it has retained its religious importance for Judaism. Religious and non-religious men can always be seen praying and worshiping at the holiest Jewish site, the Western or "Wailing Wall," a remnant of the wall of the Second Temple; ultra-Orthodox Jews in their black garments and soldiers in uniform stand side by side peacefully, while women pray separately. No one can say exactly what unites them as Jews. Since it is neither religious teaching nor the secular state, it is most probably the feeling of belonging to a community that has shared the same destiny for thousands of years.

It is impossible to say exactly how many Jews there are today. Present day estimates vary between thirteen and eighteen million in approximately 112 countries. Roughly 4.3 to 4.7 million live in Israel, forming about eighty percent of the total population of the country. Since 1989 more than half a million Jews from the former Soviet Union have immigrated to Israel; their integration demands considerable effort.

3. The Diversity of Christianity

Although Christians and Jews have a similar relationship to the Holy Land, there are differences. In reading the Old Testament of the Christian Bible, Christians recognize the Holy Land as the place where God entered into a covenant with the people of Israel, a covenant never broken. Christians are aware of their own unbreakable spiritual link to the Jewish people, and of their common roots. In Psalm 87, Christians also remember Zion when they pray: "all my springs are in you" (v. 7) or ". . . and of Zion it shall be said, 'This one and that one were born in it'" (v. 5).

Christians, however, also find evidence of their own history in the Holy Land, a history no longer related to Judaism. The New Testament speaks of Galilee and Judah as places where Jesus of Nazareth lived and preached the Gospel. According to the gospels, Jesus was born in Bethlehem, grew up in Nazareth and lived in Capernaum until he first appeared before his people. His life ended in Jerusalem. It was on Mount Zion that Jesus ate the Last Supper with his disciples. The Mount of Olives with its Garden of Gethsemane (Hebrew: oilpress), the *Via Dolorosa* along which he carried his cross, and Golgotha (Hebrew: place of skulls), where Jesus was crucified and buried, are all venerable places of worship reminding us of the suffering and death of Christ. From Jerusalem the message of his resurrection went forth to the world. Because Christians discover traces of the four gospels all over the country, Jerome, one of the fathers of the church, named it "the fifth gospel"; here more than anywhere else for Christians the names, people, and events in the Bible come alive—from here they can really "go away blessed."

Numerous reports from ancient times to the present reveal how for centuries pilgrims have been drawn to the Holy Land to fill their faith with new life at the very source of their religion. Unfortunately, Christians have also misinterpreted the meaning of pilgrimage: for example, during the crusades Christian armies turned to violence in the name of God and inflicted terrible bloodshed on Muslims and Jews in Jerusalem. Not even St. Francis of Assisi's demonstration of good will during the bloody battles in 1219—when he made great efforts to bring peace between the crusaders and the Muslim Sultan—could compensate for the suffering they caused.

Christians traveling to the Holy Land today should bear in mind the words of Pope Paul VI: the Holy Land should not be regarded as a museum. A visit there should not only be a nostalgic look at the past but also an opportunity to perceive the diversity, richness, and difficulties of the Holy Land, as well as Judaism today, the Islamic community, and the various Christian churches—in fact, it is here that many Christians first notice how many different kinds of Christian churches there really are. Nowhere else in the world do they survive in such close proximity and nowhere else in the world is there still sometimes such animosity between them. Here, where more than anywhere else they could present a shining example of the one and only all-embracing holy ("catholic") church, living in amicable diversity, they are a divided minority in a divided land.

During the first centuries the Christians who settled in the Holy Land differed in their mother tongue and origins, but not in their faith. Greeks, Latins, Egyptians ("Copts"), Ethiopians, Syrians, and Armenians, despite their different customs and ways of worshiping, considered themselves as belonging to the one and only church of Jesus Christ. This situation only lasted until the fifth century, when for the first time Christendom in Jerusalem was divided. Further oppositions and divisions, arising out of different circumstances, followed in the centuries to come. Today in Jerusalem there are, besides a number of smaller ecclesial families, four major churches: the ancient Eastern rites, the Orthodox, the Catholics, and the Reformed Churches.

- Following a decision of the Council of Chalcedon in 451, the ancient Eastern churches separated from those of the West. They could not accept the council's doctrine that the nature of Jesus Christ is both divine and human, believing only in his divinity ("Monophysitism"). This and other differences in teaching, as well as the gradual splitting up of the Roman empire into Western (Latin/Greek) and Eastern units (in the lands of the eastern Mediterranean), led to the first division of Christendom in the Holy Land. Fortunately, there is an intensive dialogue being conducted between the Catholic Church and the churches of the Middle East, including the Syrian (St. Mark Friary, close to the Jaffa Gate), the Armenian (St. James Cathedral), the Ethiopian (in the New City), and the Coptic (close to the Church of the Holy Sepulchre). This dialogue is bringing them together in their Christian belief and enabling them to live in ecumenical friendship.
- Religious disputes about the Holy Spirit, dissension about the Eucharist, disagreement about the dates of Christmas and Easter, and political arguments between the Roman and Byzantine empires were all reasons for the Latin and Greek Orthodox churches to sever their religious ties in 1054 and go their separate ways. Since then both the Latin-oriented Western church, centered in Rome, and the Orthodox churches exist in eastern Mediterranean countries. The Greek Ortho-

dox Church, which ranks highest in the family of Orthodox churches, shares the ownership of the Church of the Holy Sepulchre—known to them as "The Church of the Resurrection"—with the Armenian Church and the Franciscan Custody. Russian and Rumanian Christians belong to this Orthodox family as well, and Syrians and Copts in Jerusalem also worship in the Church of the Holy Sepulchre.

- The Catholic Church in the Holy Land consists mainly of two groups: the Latin and the Uniate churches. Those belonging to the Western churches are called "Latins" in Jerusalem because of their use of Latin in the liturgy. Since 1987 their bishop, who was granted the rank of patriarch in the nineteenth century, has been a Palestinian Christian. Among the important Catholic institutions in Jerusalem are the Franciscan Custody, the pilgrim hospice "Notre Dame," and the Ecce Homo Church of the Zion Sisters in the *Via Dolorosa,* all of which seek to care for the Latin pilgrims. The ecumenical work of the Benedictine monks of *Dormitio Mariae* (The Dormition of the Virgin Mary) on Mount Zion is especially significant. The abbey is a forum for dialogue between the divided Christian churches and among Christianity, Judaism, and Islam, and a place where young theology students can gain significant insights and experience in just one academic year.
- Efforts to reunite the Christian churches, after the Eastern and Western churches split in 1054, were only partially successful, and did not reestablish the unity of the churches. Instead, the "Uniate churches" evolved, recognizing the Pope as their spiritual head but retaining their own Orthodox rites and customs, and also admitting married priests. As a result one finds in the country today a Greek-Catholic Church whose members are called "Melkites," a Syrian-Catholic Church whose members are called "Maronites," as well as other small communities of Oriental Catholics who, since their founding, have sometimes increased the tension between the Eastern and Western churches. It remains to be seen whether one day they can be a bridge of mutual understanding, since they know both churches equally well.
- The Christian presence in the Holy Land was made still more complex when, in the nineteenth century, various European powers tried to secure a foothold in Jerusalem for their own churches. With the help of Prussia and England, Protestants and Anglicans came

to the Holy Land. The Protestant center is in the Church of the Redeemer in the Old City, while the Anglicans own Christ Church and St. George's Cathedral. Both churches maintain several pilgrim houses throughout the country. Besides these churches, Baptists, Mennonites, and Quakers are also to be found.

- Special mention should be made of the small Roman Catholic community of Hebrew-speaking Christians, which came into being in 1948 and at present has about fifteen hundred "Jewish Christians" who worship in Hebrew in Jerusalem or in their communities in Haifa and Beersheva. As Jews who have become members of the church, they would like to be a sign in the Holy Land of Christian solidarity with Israel. According to Israeli law, however, they have relinquished their Jewish identity by converting from Judaism to another religion.

Religious intolerance, national conflicts, ignorance despite close proximity, economic jealousy, mutual missionary activities with the promise of material advantage, and bitter disputes among the six Christian communities associated with the Church of the Holy Sepulchre have often been the reason for hostility among the Christian communities. It is only in recent years that mutual understanding has grown and an ecumenical way of thinking is slowly gaining ground.

The native churches in Israel today are pitifully poor; the economic and social status of the (mainly Arabic speaking) Christians is below the level of the average Israeli, and jobs for them are scarce. Many of these Palestinian Christians feel discriminated against in two ways: as Arabs in Israel they do not have the same rights and opportunities in life as the Jewish Israelis, and as Christians they are often viewed with suspicion by their mostly Muslim Arab compatriots. They not only form a small minority—residing especially in Jerusalem, Bethlehem, Ramallah, and Nazareth—but they also belong to different churches. In recent years, despite suitable professional qualifications, many Palestinian Christians—and even more so Christians living in the Arab states—have left the country because of the unsatisfactory living conditions. In 1948 there were roughly 50,000 native Christians in Jerusalem; today there are fewer than 10,000. Should this trend continue, native Christians will soon be extinct in the country where Christianity first began—in fact, the remaining Christians there today are already referring to the Holy Land as the Diaspora.

The roughly three thousand Christian foreigners in the country are for the most part either members of religious orders, high-ranking clergy, priests, staff members of embassies, or church employees. They come from countries all over the world. Religiously and politically things are not at all easy for them: if they show solidarity with Israel they lose the trust of Palestinian Christians, while if they defend the rights of Palestinian Christians they are in conflict with the state of Israel.

In 1997, according to estimates, about 160,000 Christians belonging to forty different churches were living in Israel and in the autonomous Palestinian territories. Their number varies between two and three percent of the total population. About fifty-two percent of these are Catholics (thirty percent Melkites, sixteen percent Latins, six percent Maronites), thirty-seven percent are Greek Orthodox, and of the remainder there are between one-half of one percent and two percent each of Armenians, Copts, Syrians, Ethiopians, Lutherans, Anglicans, and others.

4. Islam and its Sanctuaries

Christians visiting the Holy Land soon notice that it is home to many Muslims and from a religious point of view it is very important for Islam. Men can be seen wearing traditional Muslim clothes and women are veiled. In many places one hears the sound of the muezzin calling the faithful to prayer, and everywhere there are beautiful mosques to admire. Since the beginning of Islam, which is based on the doctrine of devotion and submission to God's merciful will, Jerusalem has played an important role for this third monotheistic religion. It was founded when Mohammed (570–632), although unable to read and write, received from the angel Gabriel the Qu'ran—the sacred text containing God's revelations to him—and then spread the message of the one God (Arabic *Allah*) to his compatriots in Mecca and Medina. Since then Muslims have considered the Qu'ran to be the only true word of God. Traditionally, Mohammed is one of the great biblical prophets, from Adam to Moses and Jesus—for Islam, he is the chief and last prophet. Islam maintains many biblical traditions in its faith, ethics, and customs, and thus in the Qu'ran Abraham is the first Muslim to be moved by God, and Jesus and the Virgin Mary are highly honored. Although Judaism and Christianity are respected as bearers of Holy Scriptures, they are also accused of falsifying them. Even during Mohammed's lifetime there were bitter fights between Muslims and Jews, since the latter refused to convert to Islam. Mohammed then instructed Muslims to pray toward Mecca *(Kibla)* during their obligatory daily prayers rather than toward Jerusalem.

In 636, four years after Mohammed's death, Palestine was taken by the Prophet's soldiers, and in 638—only two years later—Jerusalem became the third most important Islamic city after Mecca and Medina. As early as the end of the seventh century the Dome of the Rock was erected here; it was only given its fascinating appearance by talented Islamic artists some time later. Its location—which is also said to be the place where Abraham, the father of the Jewish people, was prepared to sacrifice his son, Isaac—and its architecture were designed to prove Islam superior to Judaism and Christianity. With its great dome it is a reminder of the nearby Church of the Holy Sepulchre, the site of the death and resurrection of Jesus. According to an old Islamic story, hinted at in the seventeenth *Sura,* this is where Mohammed ascended to heaven to meet Abraham, Moses, and Jesus, who are honored by Muslims as precursors of the last prophet, Mohammed. The Dome of the Rock therefore became an Islamic place of pilgrimage, but not of prayer; prayers are said in the nearby Al Aqsa mosque, on the site of the old rock (*Haram al-Sharif* or "noble sanctuary"). These two sanctuaries are among the most magnificent sights of the city and are, from a religious point of view, as important for Muslims all over the world as the Wailing Wall is for Jews and the Church of the Holy Sepulchre for Christians.

After Palestine was taken by Islam, many ancient Jewish holy places became Islamic. Among these were the graves of Abraham, Isaac, and Jacob in Hebron, Rachel's and Joseph's graves near Nablus (Sichem), Samuel's grave near Jerusalem, and the site not far from Jericho where, according to Muslim tradition, Moses is buried. Since these are all traditionally sacred Jewish sites as well, there are often clashes here between Muslims and Jews, who both react very sensitively if they feel religiously offended, releasing emotions that still today lead to malicious acts and even bloodshed.

- Almost all Muslims in the country are Sunni. They believe in the Qu'ran and also in the *Sunna* ("origin, custom") in which Mohammed sets the example for the behavior and speech of Muslims.

- The Shiites, a much smaller branch of Islam, are hardly apparent in the country. The Druse (180,000), an ancient splinter group of Shiites, live on Mounts Hermon and Carmel. Their chief sanctuary is the grave of Jethro, Moses' father-in-law (Exod 3:1; 4:18), near Tiberias; the recognition of God, redemption, and reincarnation is an important part of their esoteric doctrine. The Bahai religion broke away more recently from the Shiites and was established in Persia in the nineteenth century. They have a magnificent world center in Haifa and believe their faith, which combines elements from various religions in its rituals and doctrine, is the fulfillment of all world religions. At first they were persecuted by the Muslims who believed them to be apostates of Islam; they are still in jeopardy in Iran today.

With its 730,000 followers, amounting to fifteen percent of the population, Islam is the second largest religion in Israel today, after Judaism, and well ahead of Christianity. In the autonomous Palestinian territories, which contain only a small remnant of Jewish settlers and Christian Palestinians, Islam is dominant, with a total of ninety-three percent of the population.

II. Problems

1. Jews and Christians: From Biblical Times to Today

Jesus of Nazareth was a Jew and his first followers were Jewish. He is completely embedded in Jewish culture; he refers to the God of Israel as his Father and respects the entire body of Jewish religious law (Torah). He accepts the Jewish Holy Scriptures without question and interprets them with authority. It is only against a Jewish background that he can be fully understood. Christianity therefore has its roots in Judaism, and the church is forever inextricably bound to the Jewish religion.

But despite all this there were still serious disputes between Jesus and the Jews of his time. These, at first purely domestic conflicts, were caused by doubts that Jesus was correctly interpreting the Torah, whether he was indeed the Messiah prophesied, or whether believing in him was obeying God's law. Although his Jewish followers were convinced of this, the majority of Jews were in doubt. When, after his death, his followers preached the Gospel to both Jews and non-Jews, no longer heeding the

Torah, what was at first a disagreement among Jews alone became a dispute between Christians and Jews, and between church and synagogue.

As early as the New Testament Christians were blaming Jews for the death of Jesus, leading the Church to accuse the Jews unjustly of being "the murderers of God"; Christians also called the Jews stubborn and shortsighted for not following the Gospel of Jesus, which finally led to discrimination and segregation and the start of centuries of Christian hatred and contempt for Jews.

The Old Testament was no longer read without prejudice. Compared to the loving and forgiving Christian God, the God of Israel became a God of hatred and revenge. It was said both that the First Covenant had come to an end, and that the church had inherited it from Israel. These and other allegations intensified prejudices that, all too often, resulted in social discrimination and the bloodthirsty persecution of Jews. Christian rulers passed anti-Semitic laws, confiscated Jewish property, vandalized synagogues, accused the Jewish minority of committing serious crimes, and slighted their dignity; in sermons and religious education Judaism was scorned. Even during the last century, when Nazi racists attempted to exterminate the Jews, the churches—despite God's commandment to "love your neighbor"—did not come to their aid often enough. It was only after almost six million Jews had lost their lives during the *Shoah* (destruction, catastrophe) that Christians slowly began to realize what had happened to the Jews. Since then churches have taken steps to render more justice to Judaism.

A Jewish-Christian dialogue was initiated, in the course of which both sides got to know each other better, the church began to realize past mistakes, old prejudices were uncovered, Christians became aware once more of the roots of their religion in Judaism, and the identity of Judaism was seen in a new light. For Catholics it was the Second Vatican Council (1962–1965) that broke new ground with its declaration *Nostra aetate* (1965), which showed the church the way to a new awareness of Judaism. Pope John Paul II, pursuing the suggestions of the Council, became the first pope in church history to visit a synagogue, in Rome in 1986, and in 1993 he finally extended diplomatic recognition to the state of Israel. In Germany the discussion group "Jews and Christians," organized by the Central Committee of German Catholics, has, since 1971, sought to improve the relationship between Christians and Jews.

2. The State of Israel and Christianity

Since its foundation, the state of Israel has gradually rebuilt and impressively changed the face of the country, which had been neglected under many years of Turkish rule. These efforts have earned the Israelis admiration and respect, but, more importantly for Christians, the very existence of the state of Israel raises fundamental questions that need to be answered. The fact that it does exist enables Christians to clearly identify Jews with the country and with Jerusalem.

There is nothing in theology or history to show that the land of Israel is as important for the identity of Christians as it is for that of Jews, nor is any Christian claim to this land justifiable. Christians can only welcome the fact that Israel has become a safe place of refuge for hundreds of thousands of survivors of the *Shoah*. For many Christians the gathering of the Jewish people is proof of God's blessing. "The permanence of Israel (while so many ancient peoples have disappeared without trace) is a historic fact and a sign to be interpreted within God's design" (Vatican Commission for Religious Relations with Jews, *Notes on the Correct Way to Present the Jews and Judaism in Preaching and Catechesis in the Roman Catholic Church*, June 24, 1985). Christians are bound to respect the right of the Jewish people to live in Israel in peace and security, even if they view Israel's current politics with a critical eye.

For many years Catholics in particular were asked by their Jewish partners in dialogue why the Catholic Church withheld international recognition of the state of Israel. Unable to accept the most common reasons, such as the uncertainty of the status of Jerusalem and territories under Israeli control since 1967, and openly expressing the suspicion that it was ultimately due to theological prejudices in the Catholic Church, they argued that the words of the Second Vatican Council should be followed by deeds. But it was forty-five years after the foundation of Israel, on December 30, 1993, that the Holy See complied with the wish of the Jewish state and signed a *Fundamental Agreement* with Israel. Its preamble refers to "the single character and universal significance of the Holy Land," draws attention to "the unique nature of the relationship between the Catholic Church and the Jewish people," and recalls the "historic process of reconciliation and growth in mutual understanding and friendship between Catholics and Jews." In the first article the state of Israel and the

Holy See affirm their "continuing commitment to uphold and to serve the human right to freedom of religion and conscience." In the second article the Vatican reiterates its "condemnation of hatred, persecution and all other manifestations of anti-Semitism directed against the Jewish people and individual Jews anywhere, at any time and by anyone." Further articles affirm the right of the Catholic Church to have religious organizations in Israel and to control their religious, moral, and social affairs. It also deals with questions concerning the status of the holy sites, pilgrimages and institutions, and cultural and academic exchanges. In Article XI both parties undertake to encourage peaceful settlements of conflicts between states and nations; the Vatican further vows not to involve itself in short-term conflicts, particularly those concerning controversial borders and territories.

This Israeli-Vatican agreement, and the resulting exchange of ambassadors in 1994, was an important step in the process of building confidence between the Jewish people and the Catholic Church. This agreement, based on the principles of mutual reciprocity and respect, deals with matters of cooperation and clarifies the legal status of the two parties. At the same time it is also a symbol to the whole world—especially the Jewish world—of the church's changing attitude toward the Jewish people and Judaism. Although it is not an agreement between two religions, it is significant for Jewish-Christian relations and will be instrumental in resolving practical problems. Since all other churches in Israel expect their interests to be considered by the Vatican's representatives, the Israeli-Vatican agreement will benefit every Christian community in the state of Israel.

After this diplomatic and political breakthrough, Catholics may have become more receptive to matters called to mind by the very existence of Israel, for example, a Jewish people that cannot be overlooked. Today's Israel would not have been possible without Judaism's ancient loyalty to tradition and faith, which enabled them to survive years of dispersal without political guidance and to protect their solidarity and identity, come what may. It is this fidelity that enabled Jews who escaped death during the *Shoah* to make a new beginning in Israel. Christians, whose communities have so far been spared such a long and agonizing survival test, could learn from the Jews' example what it means to live a life of loyalty to tradition and faith. Thus the biblical promise "he shall gain life who is justified through faith" will become clear to them (Rom 1:17; Gal

3:11; Hab 2:4). On the other hand, even loyalty to faith cannot lock itself up in an imaginary world of religious independence, surviving isolation from world politics and history. The history of the Jewish people in the nineteenth and twentieth centuries shows how religious tradition, under certain circumstances, is driven by necessity to play a political role in history. Whether or not Christian visitors approve of the state of affairs in the country today, the mere existence of the state of Israel confronts them with the necessity to recognize that a faith that has provided a minority the means to survive without state or political protection can and must continuously be associated with matters of state and politics.

3. Conflicts between Jews and Muslims

The problems between Judaism and Islam date back to the beginning of Islam when there were two contrasting trends. On the one hand Mohammed respected the religion of the Jews as "people of the Book" (the Bible). As the two religions are similar in matters of faith and ethics, Jews were treated with understanding and tolerance in countries dominated by Islam, and as religious persecution suffered by Jews was rare, Jewish-Islamic cooperation increased. On the other hand, during Mohammed's lifetime there was armed conflict in Medina causing bloodshed between Muslims and Jews, since the latter accepted neither Islam nor Mohammed as prophet. Thus began a long tradition of hostility that, with its mixture of religious fundamentalism and nationalism, has reached terrible extremes today.

For decades there have been bitter political (rather than religiously motivated) struggles between Jews and Arabs in the Holy Land, primarily over the possession of land and property, with both parties appealing to historic rights. Unfortunately, the plan drawn up by the United Nations in 1947 to create peace by dividing the country into Arab and Jewish territories foundered, and since then there have been several wars between Israel and its Arab neighbors. Although Israel was able to avert the threat to its existence and secure a homeland for persecuted Jews from various countries, life became intolerable for a large proportion of the Arab population. Thus many Palestinians today live in utter misery, suffering from poverty and unemployment, with few opportunities for vocational training. Since the *Intifada,* which started in 1987, they have taken up the struggle against Israel, with riots and labor strikes—both sides demonstrating extreme bitterness. Despite the introduction of a peace process, terrorist attacks and dubious political decisions have kept mutual fear and hatred alive today.

Although religion is not the reason for this long-lasting struggle, it does play a part. The conflict between Israel and the Arab nations is also a conflict between Judaism and Islam. Since the land of Israel has not only material but also religious value, religion lends force to Jewish and Arab nationalism, fanning the flames of hatred on both sides. To make matters worse, those who consider themselves to be particularly religious have waged a "holy war" in God's name, committing terrible acts of violence and causing immense suffering.

But there are also men and women on both sides who show no fear in fighting for peace; mothers in particular have become active. The remarkable efforts of these men and women, no matter how small, demand great courage. The most prominent victims so far in the struggle for peace have been the Egyptian President Anwar al Sadat and the Israeli Prime Minister Yitzhak Rabin, who, because of their willingness to shake hands on a peaceful compromise on behalf of their nations, were treacherously assassinated by religious fanatics. Although as yet the peaceful forces of the two religions have been unable to achieve a specific breakthrough, they still constitute the best hope for a better future.

4. Christian Visitors to Israel from Germany

To German Christians visiting Israel, the historical connection between the Nazi extermination of a large part of the Jewish population and the actual foundation of the state of Israel is quite obvious. As visitors to the Holy Land, they were preceded by those Jews for whom entry into the "land of their ancestors" was the only way to escape Hitler's mass murder of Jews in Europe. Those who try to forget the murder of Jewish men, women, and children in their native country lose the opportunity of understanding the existence of the state of Israel and the Judaism that survives in it. Such a chance is offered by a visit to *Yad Vashem* ("Memorial and Name; see Isa 56:5), the national memorial in Jerusalem for the commemoration and documentation of the victims of the Nazi regime. The records of the horror of the extermination are heartrending, the children's memorial is shocking, and the vale of destruction only a meager reflection of the immeasurable loss suffered by Jewish people. Germany and Europe have become so much poorer through the Nazi genocide of Jewish people; it is almost impossible for Christian visitors from Germany to evade the shame, sorrow, and grief. No matter how painful it is for German Christians to recollect and remember the frightful past, a visit to these memorial sites is essential for an awakening of the spiritual dimension of their journey to the Holy Land. They should perhaps see it as an obligation to do everything possible to prevent something similar from ever happening again, in the name of either Germans or Christians.

In addition to the pain they feel in recalling history, Christian visitors from Germany can be quickly provoked by the continuous political conflicts in Israel today. When meeting the country's people they are inevitably drawn into their arguments; all sides demand from them loyalty and understanding, throwing them into a serious dilemma, for no matter what their political opinion may be, they must be wary of making superficial judgments. Knowing their past history, and disapproving of violence for solving domestic or foreign political conflicts, they should become unequivocal advocates of the peace process.

III. Hope

1. Ecumenism Today

Despite their awareness of the tension and conflicts in Israel, Christian visitors to the Holy Land may experience a strengthening of their hope for peace and salvation, a hope they share with Jews and Muslims. The Jewish people have had this hope ever since Abraham first received the "blessing for the nations" and peace and salvation have smoothed the way for other nations. Christians coming to the Holy Land from a secular background become a symbol of hope themselves for the prophesied "last pilgrimage" of the nations (Isa 2:1-5; Mic 4:1-5). The Second Vatican Council referred to this mutual hope when it spoke of the day "when people will all call upon the name of the Lord to serve him with one accord" (Zeph 3:9). This eschatological hope is shared by Jews, Christians, and Muslims; for example, the Last Judgment is the basis of Mohammed's preaching and the resurrection is referred to in numerous *Suras* of the Qu'ran. In the hope for God's promised salvation, the yearnings of Jews, Christians, and Muslims come together beyond the bounds of their religions.

Despite their conflicts throughout history and today, the monotheistic religions have a particularly strong sense of ecumenism: they all believe in the one God, creator of heaven and earth, and trust in his ways for the salvation of humankind. He also revealed himself as God to Abraham, preached through the prophets, will come to judge the living and the dead, and his kingdom will have no end.

Abraham is a dominant figure for all three religions. For the Jewish people he is the first of the three great patriarchs: "Look to Abraham your father" (Isa 51:2); Christians meet him in the first sentence of the New Testament (Matt 1:1: "An account of the genealogy of Jesus the Messiah, the son of David, the son of Abraham"); he is the father of their faith: "'Abraham believed God, and it was reckoned to him as righteousness'" (Rom 4:3; see Gen 15:6), and he "was called the friend of God" (Jas 2:23; see Isa 41:8). For Islam, Abraham sets an example of obedience and devotion to God, which is why, in the Qu'ran, he is often referred to as the "first Muslim." Jerusalem is the Holy City for all three religions: since its capture by David, the conveyance of the Ark of the Covenant to the city, and the construction of Solomon's Temple there, it has been the capital city and central site of worship in Israel. Despite the destruction of the Second Temple (70 C.E.) and centuries of Jewish exile, it is still the heart of the country for Jewish people. Jews living both in the state of Israel and in the Diaspora recognize it with a new intensity as their capital city, even though it is laden with strife. Jerusalem became central in the history of the Christian churches through the suffering, death, and resurrection of Jesus in Jerusalem, the descent of the Holy Spirit on the disciples gathered there, and the formation in Jerusalem of the early church. Muslims revere Jerusalem as the site of the prophets' appeal to God, and of Mohammed's ascent to heaven.

The monotheistic religions also share basic ethical principles. Islam is based on the doctrine of submission to the will of God, which is why its followers proudly call themselves "Muslims," meaning "one who surrenders to God," just as Abraham once surrendered to God. For Jews and Christians, submission to God's will, as preached by both the prophets and Jesus, also means the necessity to change one's ways. The moral imperative is to love God and one's neighbor (see Deut 6:5; Lev 19:18; Mark

12:30-31), and at the aim is a world of justice and peace, reaching fulfillment in God's royal reign.

Interfaith meetings on social, academic, and spiritual levels are an approach to expressing the bond between Jews, Christians, and Muslims. On the social level there are joint projects, usually inspired by the Jews in the "Interfaith Coordinating Council in Israel" (ICCI), which suffered setbacks during the first *Intifada.* One of the best-known initiatives is Neve Shalom near Jerusalem, a village of Jewish and Palestinian (Muslim and Christian) families who try to live peacefully together as Israeli citizens. Besides the kindergarten and primary school, the village runs a School of Peace that, with courses and seminars, seeks to sharpen awareness of the complex Jewish-Palestinian conflict and promote understanding between Jews and Palestinians. Further interdenominational projects of the parent organization ICCI in villages and towns facilitate meetings between Jews, Christians, Muslims, and Druse.

On an academic level several groups have, since Israel's foundation, devoted their time to promoting fruitful discussion between Jewish and Christian scholars. One such group is the "Ecumenical Theological Research Fraternity in Israel." Although Muslim representatives have strong reservations about religious discussions based on Western methods, they work together on a scholarly basis in studying Islam.

On the spiritual level, Jewish, Christian, and Muslim men and women come together for discussion, to learn about their different ways of worship, and sometimes to pray together. Whereas religious discussions with Muslims are difficult, the Christian encounter with Judaism is easier, and in Israel it has a chance of becoming sustainable. Every Christian group traveling to the Holy Land should include in its program discussions with a Jewish partner and worship in a synagogue, thus enabling Christian visitors to understand anew that Christianity has its roots in Judaism, with which it is inseparably linked in faith, ethics, and worship.

Although ecumenism has encouraged dialogue within Christianity, Christian visitors to the Holy Land do not always experience ecumenism in its narrower sense, namely, as a movement to promote solidarity and unity among churches. Instead, they feel the absence of the spirit of ecumenism at the holy sites because the sites are controlled by different churches and religious services are held separately. Ecumenism appears to be more urgent in the Holy Land than in any other country, and indeed there are ecumenical initiatives, meetings, and discussions. Christian denominations in Israel are becoming more and more aware that they are living in a political and social as well as a religious Diaspora. In contrast to their past, they now value common interests more than what separates them. The Week of Prayer for Unity after the Armenian Christmas (in January) is gaining in importance. During this week the various patriarchs and bishops invite one another to religious services in their respective churches, while at the same time presenting their community and customs. The week culminates in a joint service in the room of the Last Supper, where the denominations commemorate the prophesied pilgrimage of the nations and the day of Pentecost when they were "all together in one place" (Acts 2:2). The Week of Prayer has become a symbol of the hope for unity as has, for example, the restoration and new layout of the apse over the tomb in the Church of the Holy Sepulchre in Jerusalem, which was finished in January 1997 under a joint agreement between the Greek, Armenian, and Latin Patriarchies. Thus one speaks of "ecumenism of signs" in Jerusalem.

There is a growing realization that a united Christendom in Jerusalem is of great importance to the ecumenical movement among Christian churches worldwide. There is proof of this in the 1990 "Ecumenical Pastoral Plan" of the Latin Patriarchy, which, among other things, declares that

> . . . the Church of Jerusalem, as direct descendant of the early Christian Community, has a specific ecumenical calling within the worldwide Church. . . . As the source of all religious traditions, Jerusalem's mission is to achieve concrete unity in diversity. . . . The Church of Jerusalem, as Mother of all Churches, is a symbol, a microcosm, in which both its strengths and weaknesses are present. . . .

Christians in Jerusalem have a great need and yearning for unity. Thus the images of Pope Paul VI's meeting with the Patriarchs Athenagoras and Benidictos in January 1964 in Jerusalem remain both an aspiration and an ideal. Even if these Christians feel disappointed that the hopes they once had have not yet materialized, they still desire harmony and unity. In a joint memorandum of November 14, 1994, the patriarchs, church and Christian community leaders stressed the significance of Jerusalem for Christianity and ended imploringly with: "Jerusalem is a symbol and promise of God's presence, of brotherhood and peace for humankind, especially for Jews, Christians, and Muslims, the children of Abraham."

2. Tasks at Home

The hope arising from a journey to the Holy Land should be put to the test at home in the form of an open meeting between the pilgrims and brothers and sisters from the churches and religious communities encountered during their travels. There are more than half a million Orthodox Christians in Germany today. They worship in keeping with their rites and traditions and often organize their community life with the help and hospitality of local Protestant or Catholic communities. Orthodoxy is represented in Germany by a variety of individual national Orthodox churches, most of which belong to the Greek and Serbian churches, but all of which conform to the one "Orthodox Church." They are united in their common faith, manner of worship, and rules and regulations, visibly expressed in the sacramental, communal act of divine worship, the Eucharist. Encounter with the Orthodox Church is a task extending ecumenism between Catholic and Protestant Christians to include unity between the Western and Eastern churches.

Since their deportation by the Assyrians, Babylonians, and Romans, it is the Jewish people's fate to be scattered all over the world. In accordance with the Gospel mission, "Go therefore and make disciples of all nations" (Matt 28:19), Christians have been sent all over the world to teach the word of God. For centuries, therefore, but for different reasons, Jews and Christians (whose past and future connect them with the Holy Land) have been living everywhere in the world.

Christians in Germany are always amazed that, despite Auschwitz, Jewish communities remained, and even returned to live, in the "country whose recent history is darkened by its systematic attempt to exterminate the Jewish people" (Declaration, "Our Hope," Joint Diocesan Synod in the Federal Republic of Germany, 1975). While the number of Jewish communities, with their thirty thousand members, remained relatively constant over a period of many years, they have recently grown rapidly. Many Jewish families emigrated to Germany from the countries of the former Soviet Union so that their numbers at present amount to more than eighty thousand. In some communities the numbers have multiplied many times over. Communities have either been refounded or are completely new, especially in East Germany. The seventy-five communities today face great challenges: their new members from Russia, the Ukraine, or Belarus have not been brought up in the Jewish tradition; they need lessons in Hebrew and in Jewish religion as well as help with their social and professional integration, and the communities often lack staff and space to fulfill all their duties. These challenges also offer a chance for renewed Jewish life in Germany, and this is where individual Christians or churches should assist wherever possible.

If, before setting out on their journey, Christians were to familiarize themselves with the history and presence of Judaism in their native country, and possibly call on Jewish communities, they would be in a better position to understand Judaism in Israel. And if they have met with Judaism in Israel, they will understand Jewish citizens at home better. Their encounter with Jewish people at home should also prove the worth of lessons learned on the journey to the Holy Land. Christian solidarity is not only spiritual; it creates contacts wherever possible and offers help wherever necessary, assisting victims of anti-Semitism and publicly protesting against hostility to Jews and the rejection of Judaism.

It is also important for those intending to travel to the Holy Land to acquaint themselves, where possible, with the presence of Islam at home. Meetings with Muslims can help to provide a better understanding of their religious devotion and their religious and social situation in Germany, which is far from easy. In this encounter, a sense of tact is absolutely necessary. The hostility toward foreigners in recent years, often resulting in horrifying murders (especially among the Turkish minority) has caused Muslims wanting to safeguard their identity to gradually withdraw from society despite their initial desire for integration. Muslim children often suffer from social isolation and rejection; Christians are therefore called upon to show signs of goodwill and to enjoy unbiased relationships with Muslim families. (For further information see Document No. 106, "Christians and Muslims in Germany," published by the German Bishops' Conference in 1993).

3. The Hallowing of the Name

It is not the sites as such to which pilgrims travel that have the quality of "holiness." In the beginning, the mission to sanctify the world and humankind went out from the Holy Land. It is this mission, and the promise of sanctification, that has given the "Holy Land" its name: "You shall be holy, for I the LORD your God am holy" (Lev 19:2). Christians returning from the Holy Land take home this mission and the promise it holds, just as the Jews took it with them wherever they were scattered in the world. Although the hope accompanying a pilgrimage is not fulfilled by simply standing on "holy ground" once, firm believers in the Bible, whether Jewish or Christian, who have seen the "Holy Land" can find new hope in the promise contained in the Covenant. The "Land of Promise" or "Promised Land" bears its name because, as an object of God's promise, it has become a visible, tangible symbol of the future promise of salvation. Accordingly, the book of the prophet Isaiah refers to the new Jerusalem as "an ensign over the peoples" (Isa 62:10) and even ventures a vision of Israel's alliance with Egypt and Assyria (Isa 19:18-25). From the Holy Land the mission and the promise of sanctification went out to the whole world; Jews and Christians know, not only in the Holy Land, but wherever they are, that they are called to sanctify the world.

Pope Pius IX and the Jews

July 21, 2000

Official Roman sources have announced that the beatification of Pope Pius IX is to be expected for September 3, 2000. From the point of view of the discussion group "Jews and Christians" of the *ZdK,* important factors speak against this, as every beatification is not only an acknowledgment of someone's personal piety and integrity, but at the same time is meant to be a sign for the church and society of today. What signal is supposed to be given through Pius IX's beatification in the year 2000? From the point of view of the discussion group "Jews and Christians," it can only mean a disavowal of all the declarations and statements made by Pope John Paul II and several Roman institutions as a followup to the Declaration of the Second Vatican Council, *Nostra aetate* (Article 4), on the relationship of the Catholic Church to Judaism.

For one thing is certain: Pius IX was an anti-Semite—not in the sense of the primitive racial anti-Semitism of the National Socialists, but in his denouncing of a supposed "Judaization of society" in religious, cultural, and economic matters, and claiming that this had to be confronted with all the means available to authoritarian officialdom.

It is true that Pius IX did loosen the existing anti-Jewish reins during the first two years of his papacy, as several remarkable initiatives show. Thus he allowed the Jews whose houses had become uninhabitable during the great flood of the Tiber in December 1846 to live temporarily outside the Jewish ghetto, and he spared the heads of Rome's Jewish community the degrading annual ceremony of submission on Carnival Monday, which had been ordered by Pope Clement IX in 1668. In addition, he dispensed the city's Jews from listening to the hated compulsory sermon in the church of Sant Angelo in Pesceria. Finally, he ordered that the wall around the Jewish ghetto in the city of Rome be torn down during the night of April 17–18, 1848, in order to proclaim that he wanted to do away with this centuries-old stone symbol of the exclusion of Jewish fellow citizens once and for all.

Unfortunately, these alleviations for the Jews only lasted a short time. As early as 1850 the pope made a radical change of course. Basically, he returned to conditions as they were in the eighteenth century. Contrary to what had been done in all other Western European states, contrary also to what had been done in the kingdom of Sardinia, where the Jews had already been given equal rights with all the Christian citizens, Pius IX restored the ghettoization of the Jews in the Papal States. This was externally evident in the fact that he had the walls of the ghetto built up again. In so doing he pushed Rome's Jewish citizens back into a situation that, at that time in Europe, still existed only in czarist Russia. He renewed the old oppression of the Jews, refusing to allow them to practice most trades and to have administrative positions. They were again forbidden to own land, and the Talmud was once again placed on the Index of Forbidden Books, so that the Jews in the Papal States did not even have free access to their own sacred writings.

Even the medieval ritual murder stories were revived in the Papal States. The Vatican's resumption of an aggressive mission to the Jews attracted considerable attention and revulsion all over Western Europe and in the United States. Ultimately, Pius IX could only imagine coexistence with the Jews on condition that, sooner or later, they would convert to the Catholic faith. In spite of everything, the number of Jewish converts remained low in the Papal States as well as in the whole of Europe; because of this, individual conversions to Catholicism were celebrated publicly as a victory of the Catholic Church over untruth, and the people concerned were rewarded with many material favors.

According to Canon Law, it was forbidden to baptize the children of Jews against the will of their parents unless there was danger of death, or one parent had abandoned the child, or the person concerned had special psychological needs. These exceptional stipulations opened wide the door to arbitrary actions. Thus it was accepted practice that, once a Jewish child had been baptized, it was no longer allowed to remain with its parents unless they also converted to Christianity.

The worst case—only one of several that became known—was the so-called Mortara Affair: on the evening of July 23, 1858, a contingent of Bolognese police broke into the home of the Jewish merchant Momolo Mortara and demanded that his six-year-old son Edgaro be handed over to them immediately. The police officer explained to the horrified parents that their son had been a Christian for a long time, as had only recently been discovered. According to sources, a Christian maid had secretly baptized the boy when he was sick in bed. Current law therefore demanded that the boy be removed from the Jewish house and brought up as a Christian. In an act of governmental kidnapping, the boy was brought to Rome and raised there as a Christian. When this procedure gave rise to a cry of indignation all over Europe, Pius IX went a step further, documenting his legal point of view in provocative fashion. He took the boy very especially under his wing, finally adopting him when he was thirteen. Later, Edgaro entered the Order of the Canons Regular of the Lateran as a novice; he became a monk in the monastery of San Pietro in Vincoli, and in honor of his adoptive father he took the name Pio. In 1873, Pio Mortara was ordained a priest, and he died at a ripe old age in 1940.

Pius IX self-righteously spurned the letters of protest from Jewish communities in Italy, England, France, Germany, the United States, and Rome, as well as diplomatic representations from Great Britain, Prussia, and Russia, and even the admonitions from the friendly states of France and Austria. Such an attitude cannot be presented as a model for people today.

After the Jews of the former Papal States and of the city of Rome had received formal legal equality with all the other citizens of the kingdom of Italy, Pius IX was so upset that he issued a series of hate-filled tirades against the Jews that simply cannot be given another public airing.

Since the Second Vatican Council, relations between Jews and Catholics all over the world have steadily improved. Pope John Paul II himself has contributed to this in a substantial way. The beatification of Pius IX would put an unbearable burden on relations between Jews and Catholics, and in particular it would raise questions about everything positive that the church has achieved in this realm during the last decades. Now, the credibility of the pope and of his church are at stake. The beatification of Pius IX would destroy a bond for which Jews and Catholics have together made great efforts for decades. On the first Sunday of Lent 2000, before the entire world, Pope John Paul II publicly expressed repentance for past crimes against the Jewish people. How is it possible, in the same year, to beatify a pope like Pius IX, whose deeds are in such stark contrast to Pope John Paul II's confession of guilt?

Jews and Christians in Germany: Responsibility in Today's Pluralistic Society

April 13, 2005

I. Jews and Christians Have Changed

1. More Jews in the Reunited Germany

a. The Period of "Packed Bags" Is Over

Compared to the size of the communities, which together number about 100,000 members, there is an astonishingly great public awareness of Jews and Jewish institutions in the German Federal Republic. In general, anti-Semitism is noticed and rejected in the strongest possible way by both the political elite and the mainstream media. Occasionally we observe an open interest in and sympathy for the development of Jewish life by our political leaders. Subtle forms of anti-Jewish hostility receive less attention by society and the media.

In general, emigrants from countries of the former Soviet Union (FSU), who since the fall of the iron curtain have experienced acceptance, brought about a big change in the Jewish community.

After World War II survivors of the *Shoah* from Eastern Europe arrived in Germany and remained there. They became the "founding fathers" and "founding mothers" of post-war Jewish communities. They were especially important for German society. In a few years, their witness will disappear. The post-war generation that grew up in Germany and their children are taking over leadership positions in the communities. Many Jews of the second and third generation born in Germany still have a sense of insecurity because of the Nazi persecution. Therefore, we must speak of trauma that spans several generations.

Concerns about possible terror attacks continue to generate fear. Consequently, for the foreseeable future all Jewish community buildings must be protected against such attacks. With the change of generation, there is a growing conviction by members of the Jewish community that defense against terrorist attacks is a concern for all Germans.

In spite of all problems the period of "packed bags," when Jews were not sure they wanted to remain in Germany, is over. Projects for building synagogues and community centers were begun and completed. There is greater public awareness of Jewish culture. The resentment by Jews outside Germany toward those Jews who have lived in Germany since World War II has been reduced. As this acceptance by the worldwide Jewish community has grown, the self-assurance of Jews who live in Germany has improved.

In summary, Judaism has begun a new life in Germany despite great difficulties—a development which no one would have dared to dream of a few decades ago. In many cities where there were no Jews, there are Jewish activities in which young Jews participate. These are signs of hope.

b. The Einheitsgemeinde *(The Unified Jewish Community Organization) No Longer Represents All Branches of Judaism*

Until the end of the 1980s, the Jewish communities in the former Federal Republic had about 25,000 members. Many Jewish communities had a high number of elderly people. Migration from countries of the FSU put an end to the threat of demographic disappearance. Thus the number of members in the Jewish communities in the German Federal Republic grew to about 100,000. Presumably, there are about another 50,000 Jews living in Germany who do not belong to the organized Jewish community. These immigrants include many young people, and their social, economic, cultural, and religious integration has become the main task of the communities. Even at present they need the help of the organized community in finding a place to live, obtaining further education, etc. These new tasks are challenges and at the same time opportunities for the future. The communities are willing to use these opportunities and to fulfill their responsibility.

Many of the Jews living in Germany are actively committed to the destiny of the state of Israel. They give intellectual and financial support to Israeli establishments. Others have a more ambivalent relationship to the state of Israel.

Since the 1990s, a new pluralism has developed within Jewish life in Germany. Before the *Shoah*, there were essentially liberal and orthodox Judaism in Germany. At present, together with these two and the secular Jews, there are also other groups. Among these are, for example, the Lubavitcher Hassidim, who do outreach work within the Jewish community. In the meantime, the "Union for Progressive Judaism," to which a number of communities belong, has obtained legal recognition by the government (1997). The Abraham Geiger College, which was founded at Potsdam University in 1999, trains Liberal rabbis. The university faculty for Jewish Studies in Heidelberg has existed since 1979.

Christian communities must become more aware of diversity in the Jewish community. False religious expectations by Christians about Jews who live in Germany must now come to an end. These expectations would include the assumption that all Jews observe the dietary laws and the Sabbath in the same way. This idea is rooted in the erroneous presupposition that only Orthodox Judaism is considered "genuine." However, Orthodox Jews constitute only a minority of world Jewry. So that Jews and Judaism are not seen as something "exotic" education is necessary to create a realistic and unbiased relationship between Jews and Christians.

The memory of the *Shoah* must also be kept alive in the future. For us and for the next generation, "the abnormal will be normal."

2. Fewer Christians Faced with Greater Tasks

Since 1979, the situation of Christians and of the churches in Germany has also changed substantially.

Looking back, the re-establishment of German unity in 1990 also represents a decisive turning point for Christians. Although Protestant Christians in particular played a large part in this change, the churches have since then continued to lose their support in society. Since 1990, the proportion of people in Germany who are non-believers, agnostics, of esoteric orientation or religiously indifferent has considerably increased. This results in a loss of influence of the churches on German society, a phenomenon which previously had been caused by pluralism, individualism, and secularization.

In spite of all their differences, this new situation should become an occasion for Jews and Christians to work together even more than in the past. These new possibilities may exist in discussions about ecological, bioethical, and socio-political issues.

Since September 11, 2001, the media have paid greater attention to the monotheist religions as political forces. At present, the threat to Western societies from Islamic terrorism absorbs all the attention. This puts considerable pressure on interfaith dialogue between Judaism, Christianity, and Islam.

Since the second Intifada in the year 2000, the conflict in the Middle East places new burdens on Jewish-Christian dialogue. Many times the widespread criticism of the Israeli government's policy goes beyond the boundaries to forms of anti-Semitism. This type of criticism many believed had been overcome. Criticism of Israeli policy by Christian partners in dialogue should always be grounded on a fundamental solidarity with the state of Israel and its people. When this is not the case, Jewish-Christian dialogue enters into a dangerous crisis.

3. Ensuring that the Fourth Post-war Generation Will Remember

The third post-*Shoah* generation of the thirty- to forty-five-year old Jews and Christians is becoming a significant factor in the dialogue. Some are very interested in giving a fresh start to historical research on the history of Jews and Christians or in theological exploration of the *Shoah*. They want dialogue without exaggerated expectations of a future "consensus."

Dialogue between the next generation of Jews and Christians offers an important opportunity to keep the memory of the *Shoah* alive. Christian and Jewish communities should foster this as much as possible. They should not let it fall behind because of problems within each community (decrease in the number of members and financial difficulties in the churches, integration and growth in pluralism in the Jewish communities). Part of this effort should be an openness to new questions that are asked about the *Shoah* by the younger generation. The death of the survivors and witnesses of the *Shoah* will make a fundamental change in the forms of commemoration and remembrance. New forms of transmission through the media and public remembrance will play an important part. It will be necessary to evaluate this process critically. At the same time it is clear that there is no substitute for personal encounters with Jewish neighbors and free dialogue between Jews and Christians about the *Shoah*. That is the only way to ensure appropriate forms of remembrance.

II. Steps Forward—in Spite of Obstacles

1. The Pope Leads the Way

The Second Vatican Council courageously gave a new direction defining the relationship between the Catholic Church and the Jewish people. By deed and word, John Paul II opened a way into the future for this change. Statements by the church magisterium as well as by Protestant churches have initiated intense theological discussion that can be summarized in a few key sentences.

- God is faithful to his covenant with the church, but equally to his covenant with the Jewish people. Therefore, Christians and Jews are both called to understand themselves as "people of the covenant" and to be a "light to the nations" (Isa 49:6; Matt 5:14).
- No catechesis of the Christian faith without teaching the living tradition of Judaism.
- No reconciliation with God without acknowledging the history of the church's sin towards the Jewish people.
- No understanding of biblical revelation without reading the Old Testament and seriously considering Jewish interpretations.

When confronted with their traditional way of understanding their faith, these statements may be confusing to Christians. A new orientation of Christian identity is required. The Central Committee of German Catholics has made many contributions to this new orientation through its discussion group "Jews and Christians." The initiatives and teachings of John Paul II and others during his pontificate deepened many of the discussion group's efforts and gave them a stronger foundation.

A main thesis in our 1979 theological statement is, "Dialogue needs contemporary partnership." This is why the church seeks dialogue with contemporary Jews and why the church wants to hear how Jews understand themselves. We are connected with one another "for God's sake." During his first visit to Germany in 1980, the pope expressed a ground rule for Catholic theology speaking in Mainz with representatives of the Central Council of Jews and the Rabbinic Conference: "The first dimension of this [Christian-Jewish] dialogue, that is, the meeting between the people of God of the Old Covenant, never revoked by God, and that of the New Covenant, is at the same time a dialogue within our church, that is to say, between the first and the second part of her Bible." In these words the pope acknowledges that the Old Testament has theological value, "since this value is not wiped out by the later interpretation of the New Testament." In the same speech he states, ". . . a second dimension of our dialogue—the true and central one—is the meeting between the present-day Christian churches and the present-day people of the covenant concluded with Moses. It is important here 'that Christians . . . should . . . learn which fundamental lines are essential for the religious reality lived by the Jews, according to their own understanding.'"

In 1974 and 1985, the Vatican Commission for Religious Relations with the Jews published two statements. The 1985 "Notes on the Correct Way to Present Jews and Judaism in Preaching and Catechesis" criticizes the widespread ignorance of Judaism's traditions and calls upon Christians to take into account these traditions "as they are professed and practiced still today." The discussion group also made a contribution to the area of school education: since 1980, the project initiated and carried out by the discussion group at the University of Freiburg, *Lernprozess Christen-Juden* (The Learning Process of Christians and Jews) has led to a revision of schoolbooks and of annotated editions of the Bible in Germany.

John Paul II's visit to the Great Synagogue in Rome in 1986 was the first visit of a pope to a synagogue. The public perceived and acknowledged it as a historical event in the Catholic Church's rapprochement with Judaism. The pope wanted to perform a symbolic act to "overcome old prejudices and to secure a wider and more complete recognition of that 'bond' and 'common spiritual patrimony' that exists between Jews and Christians." His address culminated in the words: "You are our dearly beloved brothers and, in a certain way, it could be said that you are our elder brothers." The travels of the discussion group to Jewish communities in Israel, the USA, Poland, Hungary, France, and the Czech Republic were a response to the pope's words and actions.

In 1988, 50 years after the *Reichskristallnacht* the discussion group published the statement, "After 50 years—how can we talk about guilt, suffering, and reconciliation?" It stimulated a greater response and was disseminated more widely than any of our other texts. The pope gave public expression to the long Christian history of sin through his prayer of confession at St. Peter's Basilica in the Holy Year 2000. One of the prayers for forgiveness focused on the church's relationship with the Jews who are acknowledged as "the people of the Covenant and of the blessings." This prayer was a witness to the church's desire for reconciliation. The pope's pilgrimage to the Holy Land which followed also had great symbolic significance. He visited Yad Vashem in Jerusalem, the memorial to the six million Jews who were murdered. At the Western Wall, he left a paper with a prayer, whose text is identical to the one in St. Peter's: "God of our ancestors, you chose Abraham and his descendants to bring your Name to the nations. We are profoundly saddened by the behavior of those who, throughout history, caused your children to suffer. In asking for your forgiveness, we wish to commit ourselves to a life of authentic brotherhood with the people of the Covenant."

2. Obstacles on the Path

Unfortunately, there have been a number of events over the past years which cause us to lament and do not fit into a completely positive development. We offer three examples.

The discussion group criticized the *Catechism of the Catholic Church*, published in 1992. It is true that it does not lag behind the Council's statements about the Jews when it speaks directly about Judaism, but it does not fulfill the expectations that must be brought to a catechism in our time. Certainly, it is not consciously anti-Jewish, but it is a-Jewish, that is, it is a document that does not take the Jews sufficiently into consideration. It is clear that the *Catechism* has difficulty in acknowledging post-biblical Judaism as an independent entity alongside the church in salvation history, and in many passages it talks about the church as if Judaism did not exist, even though the subject at hand requires that it speak of the church's bond with Judaism.

The Vatican statement "We Remember: A Reflection on the *Shoah*" (1998) speaks of the historical background of anti-Semitism, the *Shoah*, and newer forms of anti-Semitism. The discussion group did think it was correct to distinguish between anti-Judaism and anti-Semitism and to recall Christianity's historical guilt. But it criticized the questionable theological distinction between the guilt of its members and the holiness of the church, which remains untouched. In summary, the discussion group saw a tendency towards apologetics in the way history was presented, and considered this as a step backwards in comparison with the 1988 statement of the German and Austrian bishops, "*Die Last der Geschichte annehmen*" (Accepting the Burden of History), and the 1997 statement by French bishops.

The discussion group criticized the simultaneous beatification of the two popes, Pius IX (1846–1878) and John XXIII (1958–1963), who were so different in their church policies. The difference seems to serve two opposing tendencies within the church. Whereas John XXIII convened the Second Vatican Council and worked personally for a renewed relationship of the church with the Jews, Pius IX, the pope of the First Vatican Council, engaged in overt anti-Jewish statements and actions. The discussion group was not alone in its praise for John XXIII and its criticism of Pius IX.

3. Christians and Jews Read the Same Bible in Different Ways

Since the Second Vatican Council's Dogmatic Constitution *Dei verbum*, there has been a new awakening in Catholic biblical theology. Official statements by the Pontifical Biblical Commission took the new exegetical insights into account. Above all, *The Jewish People and Its Sacred Scripture in the Christian Bible* (2001) is to be mentioned. Based on earlier statements, it says: "Christians can and ought to admit that the Jewish reading of the Bible is a possible one, in continuity with the Jewish Sacred Scriptures from the Second Temple period, a reading analogous to the Christian reading which developed in parallel fashion. Both readings are bound up with the vision of their respective faiths, of which the readings are the result and expression. Consequently, both are irreducible." Israel's refusal to say "Yes" to Jesus of Nazareth can also be acknowledged by Christians as fidelity to Jewish tradition. In the same way, Jewish fidelity to their own Sacred Scriptures and the Jewish hope of redemption can be acknowledged as theologically valuable for Christians. The document correctly emphasizes that the Christian understanding of the Old Testament is based on the insight that human speech has multiple dimensions; therefore the plurality of textual interpretation is at the foundation of biblical interpretation.

Jewish scholars have helped Christian theologians and religious educators to come to a better understanding of Judaism in its living diversity. For many years commentaries on the Hebrew Bible have been published, in which Jewish experts have collaborated. For Christian readers, rabbinic ways of understanding have shed new light on the books of the Bible. Since 1973 *Jüdische Schriften aus hellenistisch-römischer Zeit* (Jewish Writings of the Hellenistic-Roman Period) has been published. The writings of the Septuagint are given a very important place in the series, because all the authors of the New Testament knew these texts and their theological ideas. Many misunderstandings in Christian-Jewish dialogue happen because Jews and Christians read their scriptures in different versions. For Jews only the Hebrew has authority. Since antiquity Christians read the Old and New Testament in Greek. Many of the ideas in the Greek version were transmitted by Hellenistic Judaism. The study of Greek-speaking Judaism facilitates understanding between Jews and Christians. In interpreting the New Testament, there is more care in avoiding anti-Jewish clichés and understanding the Jesus movement as a movement of reform within the Judaism of its time. In this way the problems that arise from reading the Bible while ignoring Judaism can be avoided.

4. "Dabru Emet"—*Jewish Scholars Enter New Territory*

Over the past decades, in spite of several steps backward, Jews have played a substantial part in bringing about a surprisingly positive development in the relationship between Christians and Jews.

- In the Jewish-Christian discussion group of the Central Committee of German Catholics (ZdK), Jews and Christians discuss current religious, theological, historical, and political issues.

- For many years in English-speaking countries and beyond there has been cooperation between Christians and Jews with respect to social and political tasks.
- On various occasions, national and international Jewish organizations have positively acknowledged the statements and actions of the Christian churches.

The statement "*Dabru Emet*—Speak Truth" (September 10, 2000), goes one step further. The four authors and more than three hundred co-signers representing a broad spectrum of approaches to Judaism did not claim to possess any binding authority within the Jewish world. It is clear to many Jews that "*Dabru Emet*" has not provoked much positive response, and has been strongly criticized.

Dabru Emet enters new territory. It expresses the hope that more Jews will engage with Christians in theological dialogue.

Dabru Emet suggests:

- There are points of convergence and agreement between Jews and Christians. It states very clearly that both worship the same God, draw authority from the same book, the Bible, acknowledge the moral principles of the Torah, and have a common responsibility for the world.
- *Dabru Emet* does not avoid difficult issues. There are some differences between Jews and Christians which will remain until the end of time, e.g. the meaning of God, the Bible, and salvation. The document also clearly presents the difficult relationship of the churches to National Socialism.
- The text clearly states that Jews expect Christians to stop a specific mission to the Jews and to acknowledge their religious autonomy.
- *Dabru Emet* concludes with the hope that Christians and Jews will work together for justice and peace.

For these reasons *Dabru Emet* can provide an important impetus to the development of the Jewish-Christian relationship.

III. Issues of Continuing Controversy

1. God's Covenant with Israel Was Never Revoked

Whereas in the past the church taught indiscriminately that there was no salvation outside of the church and without Christ ("*extra ecclesiam nulla salus*"), in *Nostra aetate* the Second Vatican Council adopted the biblical belief that God wants the salvation of all (1 Tim 2:4), even of the whole world (John 3:17). Therefore, verses of Scripture like "No one comes to the Father except through me" (John 14:6; similarly: Acts 4:12; differently: Matt 7:21) should be re-assessed. This changed attitude of the church led to a new approach to all world religions. After Vatican II the unique status of Judaism was not recognized in a sufficient way and it was put on the same level as the world religions.

The discussion group rejects the tendency to diminish the unique nature of Judaism. It affirms Christianity's distinctive and non-negotiable relationship with the "Israel of God," with pre-Christian and post-biblical Judaism. Support for this argument may be found in chapters 9–11 of the Letter to the Romans, where the apostle Paul says that God does not revoke his promises (Rom 9:4). Paul is convinced that his proclamation is identical to that of the prophets (Rom 1:2). Jews and non-Jews are saved by faith alone (Rom 1:16f.). In the end, God will have mercy on all (Rom 11:32). That is valid both for Israel and for the nations.

Although Paul sees the bridge to the salvation of the nations in God's covenant with Noah and Abraham, he does not ignore the significance of the covenant at Sinai (Exod 19–20) or of the new covenant for Israel announced by the prophet Jeremiah (Jer 31:31-34). God promises to be faithful to all these covenants and bring them to fulfillment. Paul emphasizes that Israel continues to possess the covenants, the Torah, and the worship (Rom 9:4). Thus God's promises remain valid, regardless of whether Israel comes to faith in Jesus or not.

These words provide a foundation for Pope John Paul II's teaching about the "covenant never revoked." They are appropriate for emphasizing God's fidelity to the chosen people, which extends to contemporary Judaism.

However, Paul did not think that this reflection solved all the problems in the relationship between the early Christian communities and the "Israel of God." At the end of his reflections, he referred to God's inscrutable wisdom and ways of salvation (Rom 11:33-36). For this reason, contemporary Jewish-Christian dialogue should not attempt a universal resolution to theological problems. The dialogue contributes to the kinship between Jews and Christians who know and praise God's fidelity. This bond is unique among religions.

2. No More Missionizing of Jews!

Today we must gratefully acknowledge that neither Jews nor Christians are excluded from salvation. Paul states that God includes Jews and non-Jews in his mercy, each in a different way. It is God who opens up the way and the understanding of the gospel. That is why the discussion group emphatically expresses the conviction that there be no specific mission to the Jews.

Along with important biblical reasons, there are also historical grounds for this position. Throughout history, missionary work among the Jews was linked to oppression and violence. Missionary activity frightened large parts of the Jewish people. This terrible history alone sufficiently explains and justifies the contemporary rejection of the missionizing of Jews. It should have become clear to Christians that Jews resisted Christian missionizing. This opposition brought many disadvantages for the Jews. It was the firm conviction of the Jews that the life of the Torah provided their own way to God.

A firm rejection of a specific mission to the Jews does not imply that Jews and Christians should isolate themselves from one another. On the contrary, the absence of missionizing allows both communities to speak freely about their beliefs. Paul says that "all Israel will be saved" (Rom 11:26f.) when the redeemer comes out of Zion. Christians can rejoice that Jews have their own way to salvation, and not feel compelled to offer their hope for redemption to Israel.

3. What Separates Jews and Christians Must Also be Part of the Dialogue: Jesus Christ

Belief in Jesus as the Messiah is alien to Judaism or is even considered erroneous. Is it possible to build new bridges between the two faith groups based on Jesus? The discussion group believes this to be possible on two conditions:

- According to Christian faith, Jesus Christ is "the Yes and the Amen" (2 Cor 1:20) of God's irrevocable fidelity to Israel and to the whole world.
- Nevertheless, there is salvation for Jewish people who do not believe in Jesus as the Christ because of God's covenant with them.

The apparent contradiction in the two statements can be resolved only by the infinite wisdom of God (cf. Rom 11:25-36). According to Franz Rosenzweig, this aporia can only be determined when the first word (of creation) has become the final word (of redemption).

For Christians Jesus is the center of faith. For Jews the question of Jesus is not part of their understanding of God. Nevertheless, our discussion group asserts that Jesus must have a place in Jewish-Christian dialogue. Because of its Christology the Christian side must be aware of misunderstandings. This means that the Christian interpretation of Jesus as savior must include more than just a consideration of the historical Jesus. On the other hand, it must develop more than a dogmatic Christology that speaks of the incarnation of God as if Jesus replaced the Creator God of the Old Testament. The face-to-face relationship of Jesus with the God of Israel and, at the same time, Jesus' union with the Father (cf. John 17:11) are the basis of Christian teaching on the Trinity. According to Christian faith, these concepts do not contradict belief in the one God. The Council of Chalcedon (451) plays a decisive role in defining the concept of the incarnation. The council states said that Jesus Christ is fully divine and fully human (*vere Deus* and *vere homo*). Accordingly, the Word of God (*Logos*) can really be heard in the human being Jesus, in his life, his person. Therefore, the humanity of Jesus may not be diminished. But on the other hand, this self-emptying of God does not mean that God has not communicated himself in Jesus. Therefore, divinity and humanity maintain their specific nature and may not be melted into one. In order to avoid misunderstandings in the dialogue with Jews, Christians must maintain the clear formula of their early profession of faith.

In our continuing conversation with Jews, the humanity of Jesus remains particularly significant. This is because it is Jesus who offers himself unto death both to the God of Israel and to the human being in need of salvation. He is savior because he teaches us to walk on the path of salvation. But he is more because as fully divine he lowered himself unto death.

It is he who was in the form of God and who humbled himself unto death (Phil 2:6-8). In him, the "goodness and loving kindness" of God appeared (Titus 3:4). Jesus Christ, therefore, is a sign of God's faithful promise. This goodness and loving kindness of God is illuminated in his life and in his death. In his resurrection God's fidelity is confirmed.

There are ideas in Judaism that resemble these notions of Christology. In early Rabbinic texts there are numerous examples revealing God's drawing near to humanity and the created world. However, none of these texts identifies this relationship with a human being who lived on earth.

4. The Scandal of a World Unredeemed

In the life, death, and resurrection of Jesus, Christians see the foundation of their salvation that was established by God (2 Cor 5:18f.). This faith, which Jews do not share, has been harshly tested through the unredeemed condition of the post-Holocaust world in the twenty-first century. There is still sin, suffering, and death, although Christians expect that God's Messiah should have brought an end to them. But neither Israel nor the world currently live in peace.

We turn again to Paul who first refers to this difficult problem. According to him, "all creation is groaning in labor pains even until now" (Rom 8:22). According to St. Paul, salvation in its universal fulfillment is only realized by means of hope.

Jews also have a hope for the redemption of the world. Based on God's promises they work for the repair of the world (*Tikkun Ha-Olam*). Therefore, in the light of a world unredeemed Christians and Jews find a common hope and impetus for collaboration.

This cooperation is demonstrated in the way Jews and Christians give concrete help, love, and care to those who are suffering. This common action is more important than all theological reflection on suffering and redemption. That is what the biblical commandment "to love" means. That is the message of the prophets, who became defenders of orphans and widows and publicly denounced injustice in the name of God. The Gospels continuously show how Jesus fought against suffering and injustice. On the Day of Judgment, the only valid measure for him is: "Just as you did it to one of the least of my brothers or sisters, you did it to me"

(Matt 25:40). Jesus stands in unity with the prophets of Israel (Isa 58:1-14) and his statement represents a continuity with Jewish ethics. From these biblical statements the task that is central to Jews and Christians emerges: to perceive and alleviate the suffering of others. As both communities engage in these tasks they create signs of redemption in an unredeemed world.

In the Gospel according to Matthew it says: "Not everyone who says to me 'Lord, Lord,' will enter the kingdom of heaven, but only the one who does the will of my Father in heaven" (Matt 7:21). This statement indicates that Matthew's community acknowledged that there is redemption in fidelity to Torah without referring to Jesus. For this reason then, Christians and Jews are more united by their hope in the fulfillment of redemption, than they are separated by the Christian interpretation of Jesus.

IV. Biblical Ethics Obliges us to Contribute to World Society

1. Human Dignity Must be Defended

Today Jews and Christians are faced with new tasks they have in common. Biblical ethics are an absolute criterion for the inspiration of contemporary society.

Therefore, Jews and Christians are required to oppose the use of human beings as instruments of a society that makes economic power into idolatry. The obligation for Jews and Christians to honor a day of rest, Shabbat or Sunday, points the way toward restoring human beings in the image of God. This becomes credible only when Jews and Christians cultivate a culture for this day corresponding to their faith and as a model for society.

In addition, we currently face social reforms in Germany and, as religious communities, we make it our common task to be a voice that speaks for the weak and the helpless and to insist that they live with dignity.

We will collaborate to promote the protection of human life from birth to death and oppose medical assisted suicide. However, significant differences about the issues of human life require further discussion between our communities. According to Catholic teaching, the dignity of the human person begins with conception. This belief is not shared by all Jews. Therefore, Jewish thinkers can draw different conclusions from the common biblical tradition than those of Catholic theologians with respect to the protection of the embryo. Catholic and Jewish ethics would differ with respect to prenatal and pre-implantation diagnosis and procedure. Yet, Jews and Christians agree that the dignity of the human being may not be violated. This dignity is based on the biblical idea that the human being is created in the image of God. It is supported by the constitution of the Federal Republic of Germany. Therefore, Jews and Christians are convinced that where human dignity is not respected, the constitutional state may also be threatened at its very foundation.

2. Hostility toward Jews—An Old Scandal in a New Garb

In many countries hostility toward Jews has aggressively reappeared recently. The discussion group reminds Christians that their solidarity with Jews should be self-evident. This means that actions and public statements that express hostility to the Jewish people oblige a vigorous response from Christians who should not leave the response only to the Jews.

It is necessary to analyze the causes that have led to this new hostility towards Jews. The discussion group would point to the following list: the increase in militant Islamic groups, the success of radical Rightist parties, the growth of xenophobia, the alienation of many young people and, finally, the insufficient integration of foreigners, migrants, and marginal groups.

In contemporary public discussions hostility to Jews is often linked with criticism of the state of Israel's policies. Jews properly expect people to make a distinction between the policies of the Israeli government and the Jews who are living in Germany. However, it also should be clear that criticizing the state of Israel does not mean supporting anti-Semitism.

3. An Open Conversation with Islam

Without intense dialogue between the "monotheistic religions" it is impossible to imagine that people in the Middle East or in Germany will live together peacefully. That is why the discussion group welcomes all initiatives in what is often called an "Abrahamic" or also a "trialogical" dialogue between representatives of Jews, Christians, and Muslims.

However, it must be remembered that relations between Jews, Christians, and Muslims are of a different nature. Judaism and Christianity have a special relationship with one another because they share the Hebrew Bible, which Christians call the "Old Testament." The Qu'ran, however, does not acknowledge the Old and the New Testaments as revelation, even though it refers to persons and events in them. Moreover, along with positive statements about Judaism and Christianity in the Qu'ran, there are also passages which Jews and Christians understand as distorted descriptions of their faith.

Our discussion group "Jews and Christians" desires an open dialogue with Muslims. This dialogue should not avoid theological discussion for the sake of future consent. At the outset we want to promote a dialogue that rejects discrimination against others, and that affirms religious freedom and the protection of human rights.

The Central Committee of German Catholics currently sponsors a discussion group "Christians and Muslims." At the present time our discussion group and the Christian-Muslim group have emphasized different areas of interest. We believe that collaboration should be encouraged in the future. The contents of religious traditions are often used to support the interests of small groups within the larger community. Our discussion group rejects this instrumental use of any religious tradition. In the future we want to avoid any instrumentalizing within our own communities, and we support the efforts of many Muslims towards working together and living in peace.

4. Working among the German Public and in the Schools

Bringing the new perspectives and insights from its work into the public arena remains a continuing task for our discussion group. It shall support academic conference centers working in this field and promote the ideas of Christian-Jewish dialogue in adult education, parish work, and the media. We want to give special emphasis to a more profound understanding of Judaism and relations between Judaism and Christianity in the areas of preaching and catechesis. These activities are in conformity with numerous statements of the magisterium.

Religious education has the task of introducing our youth to the results of Jewish-Christian dialogue. It is clear that initiatives of the discussion group have had a positive impact over the last decades. Curricula and schoolbooks, didactic material and the development of projects, specialized literature, media, and conferences offer teachers help that can lead to presenting the subject of "Judaism" in a responsible way. However, a lack of knowledge and understanding of Christian-Jewish topics can still be recognized among pupils and occasionally also among teachers.

At the present time, in contrast to the early days of the discussion group, about one third of all pupils do not attend religious education classes. Most of them take part in other subjects such as philosophy or *Lebenskunde/Ethik/Religion* (life/ethics/religion). Therefore, a question arises which is even more urgent: how can our schools transmit an understanding of Judaism and Christianity in classes that do not focus on religion? Teachers in all subjects will bear greater responsibility in transmitting corresponding insights and knowledge. We believe that it is impossible to understand our European culture and history without studying Jewish-Christian relations.

5. *Judaism and Christianity: A Critical Voice in Public Discussions*

The biblical commandment to love God and neighbor (cf. Deut 6:5; Lev 19:18; Mark 12:28-31) is obligatory for both Jews and Christians. Our two communities proclaim faith in One God, whom we love with all our heart, with all our soul, and with all our strength. This belief unites us above and beyond all theological differences. The human person created in the image of God (*betselem elohim*: Gen 1:26) is called to responsibility before God. According to rabbinic tradition, this responsibility is demonstrated in what the person does in the fulfillment of God's commandments. Our actions are directed toward recognizing the image of God in those with whom we live.

Today, Catholic social teaching speaks of "faith's responsibility for the world." Judaism emphasizes that being chosen by God brings with it a responsibility to foster justice and peace in the world. Therefore, Jews and Christians are required to work toward a world that reflects the image of the Creator. We are convinced that reflection and action by our communities based on our religious traditions will benefit the political and social issues that constitute the fabric of civil society.

Currently monotheism is often criticized as promoting an absolutism that engenders violence. Just the opposite is the case. As Jews and Christians we remember that our common ethical task flows from the human bond with the Creator. This link prevents us from making anything absolute that is not God. Therefore, our faith in one God obliges us to engage in criticism of idolatry and totalitarianism. In secularized societies this religious voice seems more necessary than ever.

Because ties to religious traditions have become visibly weaker in our society, it is necessary for Jews and Christians to communicate their biblical traditions in public discussions about our future. Our discussion group asserts that this task is increasingly more difficult. We must seek new partners in dialogue among people who do not belong to any religious institution or tradition but who are seriously concerned about justice and peace on earth and about the future of the world.

Therefore, Jews and Christians are both responsible for developing ways of effectively acting and speaking in an environment that is secular.

Conclusion: Together "Called to Be a Blessing for the World"

Forty years after *Nostra aetate* the discussion group acknowledges with gratitude that the Second Vatican Council's declaration has born fruit within the Christian community. Similar statements and initiatives in the churches of the Reformation have made substantial contributions. It seems that the main obstacles which separated the Christians from the Jews and which caused the Jewish people in "Western Europe" terrible suffering and bloody persecutions have been removed. The churches have condemned the accusation of Deicide, the claim that the chosen Jewish people have been rejected by God, as well as the legitimization of hatred of the Jews. We Christians have become aware of the fact that we are related to Judaism from the "root" and that we cannot understand ourselves correctly without Judaism.

This historical turning point of the Council can never be reversed. The spiritual bond, which ties together Jews and Christians, may not be torn asunder again! Thanks be to God, the message of *Nostra aetate* is understood in Germany, the land of the *Shoah*. Nevertheless, the danger of anti-Semitism remains. It still appears in Germany and other parts of the world in new forms.

For this reason the task of the discussion group "Jews and Christians" in the Central Committee of German Catholics is not yet finished. What has been accomplished so far is not enough. We reject the accusation occasionally made that we are pursuing a hobby or that we are a lobby. Christian-Jewish dialogue is not peripheral but at the center of Christian identity. We know that our society is changing. Therefore, we must reach out to a new generation of men and women who will engage the dialogue we have begun and bring their own ideas and passion.

In considering our work since 1979 we believe that our first task is to keep the memory of the *Shoah* alive in the fourth generation born after the Second World War. We must recall the causes, including the anti-Judaism within the church that led to the *Shoah*. The second ongoing task is to direct the rapprochement in the dialogue of Christians and Jews toward their common responsibility for our endangered society and world. The challenging invitation offered twenty-five years ago by Pope John Paul II in Mainz remains our task today: "Jews and Christians, as children of Abraham, are called to be a blessing for the world." We look forward to the day when Muslims, who are also children of Abraham, will join us in this task. May the Lord of history bless our work!

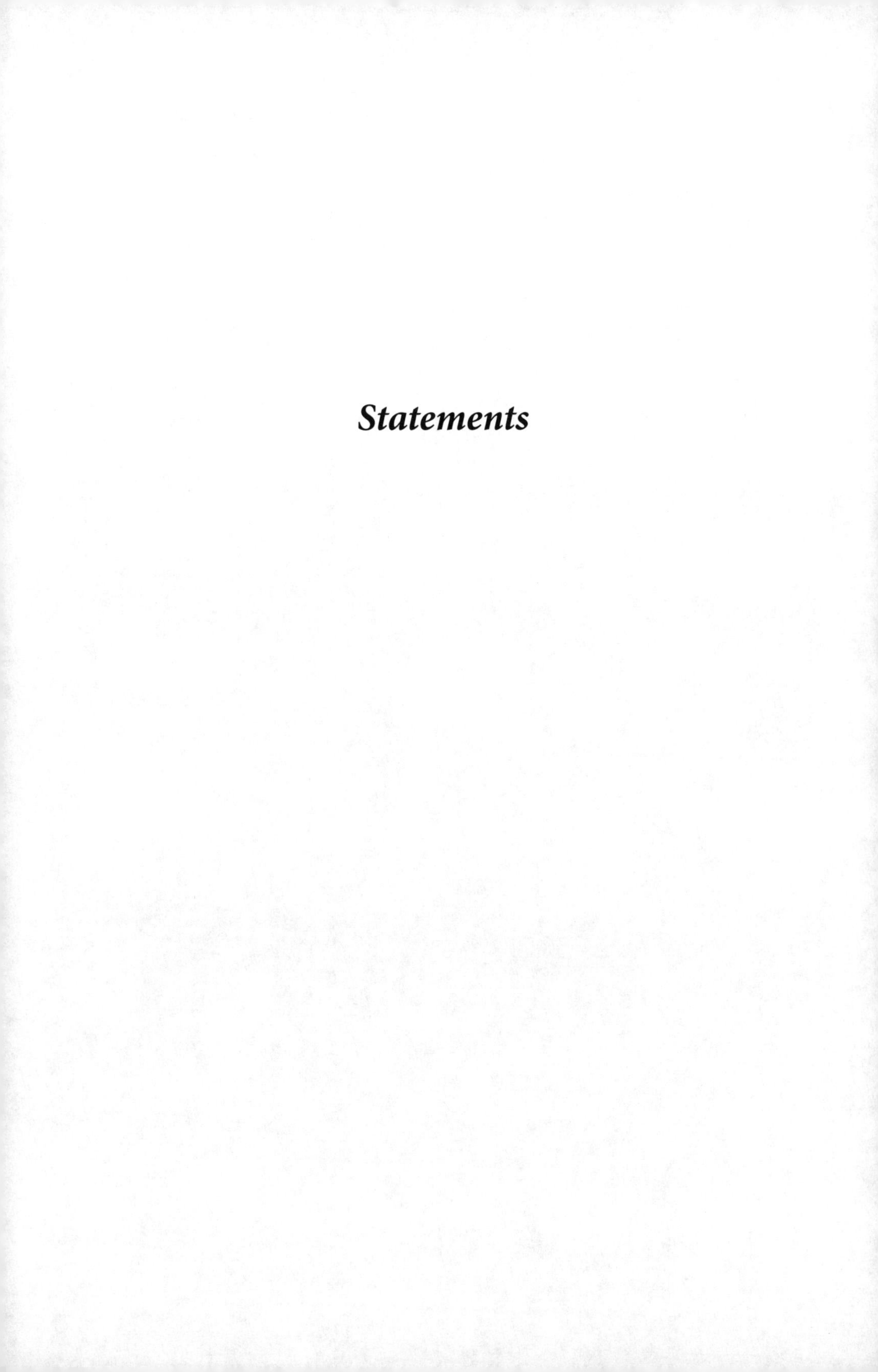

Statements

The Road Is Made by Walking

Mary C. Boys

I have read the documents from the discussion group "Jews and Christians" several times—both because they bear rereading and because I needed to refresh my memory before I could get to the long-delayed task of fashioning a response. Today as I reread them, fragments of conversation among the members of one of my courses this term echoed in my mind. So I begin with some of those echoes.

The course, "Studies in Jewish-Christian Relations," has Jews and Christians in equal numbers, a rare opportunity made possible in part by the fact that the Jewish Theological Seminary of America is located just across the street from my institution, Union Theological Seminary. Some of the Jews, most of whom are rabbinical students, are children or grandchildren of survivors, and "the *Shoah* is a deep wound that is still bleeding."[1] Most have had little opportunity to engage seriously with Christians. So, too, the Christian participants seem to have had few sustained encounters with Jews. Despite the relative newness of such situations of dialogue for both, class sessions are characterized by a remarkable candor. Class members meet not only in the formality of an academic setting but also in more informal study groups over a shared meal or a field trip of their own choosing. They contribute as well to an "open

1. Cited in "After Fifty Years: How Can We Talk about Guilt, Suffering and Reconciliation?" (above, pp. 27–41).

forum" on a class Internet site; those frank exchanges extend and refine comments made in class. The site also contains a variety of papers written by persons working in Jewish-Christian dialogue and has links to many relevant websites.

Since our class session last week focused on the Holocaust, it is not surprising that the text that touched me most deeply was "After Fifty Years: How Can We Talk about Guilt, Suffering and Reconciliation?" I see the faces of class members when I read sentences such as "During the last three years we Christians have realized anew that it is really a miracle when a Jew can grasp the hand stretched out toward him or her, after all the suffering and injustice inflicted on this people and on his or her relatives and acquaintances." Yes, not only in Germany, where the burden of the past is so heavy, but here in New York, too: facing history is an almost unbearable task. It is indeed a miracle that these Jews cross Broadway each week to engage with Christians, a miracle that friendships are forming, a miracle that trust is developing.

Last week two students prefaced their remarks with, "I may not be saying this the right way, so please do not take offense—but I need to say this." It often seems to me that we share the dilemma of "How can we talk?" Certainly, I feel this myself. For example, we studied the Gospel of John together, using as one of our commentaries the book by Adele Reinhartz, *Befriending the Beloved Disciple: A Jewish Reading of the Fourth Gospel.* Even with her frank engagement with John, how can we talk about this text—a text still sacred to the Christian members of the class, but now read with much more pain? How can we talk about this text in the present, now that we know what the history of our two traditions has been? As one of the Jews wrote in the open forum: "As the granddaughter of Holocaust survivors, the anti-Jewish rhetoric in John, no matter how justifiable in its historical context, is difficult to accept in light of more recent history. Even as I try to understand the ways in which the Fourth Gospel may be compelling to Christians, the shadow of the *Shoah* looms dark overhead."

For all the years I have studied this gospel, initially under the tutelage of my late, beloved mentor, Raymond E. Brown, nothing has had the impact of hearing from Jewish students like her. I have read scores of books and articles analyzing the anti-Jewish character of John. I am grateful for what my reading has taught me. Yet a more visceral learning comes when a student says in class: "I respect the complexity of the situation out of which this text comes. But to be the 'other' about whom it speaks is just so painful."

Thus I wish to underline the importance of talking across boundaries of difference, especially when the conversation involves difficult matters. "We have worked on what we can say together," the German discussion group writes. This work is itself a miracle—but it is indeed work.

> Walker, walker, there is no road.
> Walker, walker, there is no road.
> The road is made by walking.

So writes Spanish poet Antonio Machado. The "talk" of Jews and Christians is a walk that makes a road, but it is arduous labor.

One aspect of that labor is searching the tradition for wisdom that might help our talk become a common walk. The German discussion group provides a model for this by drawing on traditional Catholic and Jewish sources on repentance, even as they recognize the inadequacy of these sources. They rightly acknowledge that the *Shoah*—and the centuries of the "teaching of contempt" that preceded it—changed everything: "Traditional modes of behavior must be reconsidered in a new and deeper way in order to apply them to the wrong for which one community as a whole must assume responsibility toward another community to whom, as a whole, wrong has been done."

"Both must go out to meet one another; both must find the way to each other again," they write. Again, my class comes to mind. Crossing the street to one another's schools is only a beginning. So, too, meeting in a café for coffee or going to the services of the other's tradition is only a step on this journey. Yet are we not in our own small way taking the first steps toward one another that help to heal the wounds of history? Is not even a modest step a miracle? In a time when hope seems so elusive, it is vital to give thanks for every instance of finding our way to each other.

Steps Toward a New Theological and Human Awareness

Ernst Ludwig Ehrlich

Since it came into existence as a result of the *Katholikentag* (a national Catholic convention) in Trier in 1970, the discussion group "Jews and Christians" has accomplished astonishing things. It is unique of its kind in the world. At a very early point it looked at theological questions concerning Catholics and Jews and published several declarations addressing these questions; the declarations were approved by the executive committee of the *Zentralkomitee der deutschen Katholiken* (*ZdK:* Central Committee of German Catholics). Not least among the factors making this theological dialogue possible were the profound scholarly and human insights of the late bishop of Aachen, Klaus Hemmerle, spiritual director of the *ZdK,* who died all too early. The discussion group's basic document has the title: "Important Theological Issues for Jewish-Christian Dialogue." Even then, in 1979, it was obvious for the discussion group that Christian missionary activity toward Jews was absurd. Points in common and divergences are expressed unambiguously and prejudices are dismantled—for example, Christians accusing Jews of believing in "justification through works." On the other hand, Christians emphasize strict allegiance to the one God of Israel because it is precisely their faith in Jesus Christ that brings them into relationship with the God of Israel. These examples show that as we question one another the salvific significance of the other path is acknowledged to a certain extent.

The group's position on political events was also expressed, for example, in 1988, on the fiftieth anniversary of the so called *Reichskristallnacht* (Night of Broken Glass). Of course, the discussion group did not want just to make a political statement expressing its loathing for these events; rather, it also wanted to try to reflect together on guilt, repentance, and conversion. The declaration was presented to the general assembly on April 29, 1988. Participants later said that this was the *ZdK*'s most impressive and emotional meeting. Here, in a large forum, a solidarity between Jews and Catholics became visible, something that unfortunately had not existed in the past.

In 1996 the discussion group expressed its view of the new *Catechism of the Catholic Church,* regretting that the church's anti-Judaism, which is rooted in the separation of the early church from Judaism, was not mentioned. A post-*Shoah* catechism should have pointed out the history of guilt in the earlier catechisms.

> The establishment of the Carmelite convent in Auschwitz was a particular irritant in the relationship between Jews and Catholics. It took years before this annoying problem could be solved through Pope John Paul II's authoritative intervention. The discussion group's statement on the situation says: "Auschwitz must be protected from any group or institution laying claim to the truth and seeking to use Auschwitz for its own purposes." The text continues: "In memory of Auschwitz we Christians must understand . . . that we have forfeited much of our credibility because, as religious communities, we at that time—in spite of the exemplary conduct of individuals—ignored the suffering of the Jewish people."

In its statement, "Reflections on the *Shoah,*" the discussion group looked at the declaration of the Vatican Commission for Religious Relations with Jews of March 1998. It regretted not finding a clear expression of the church's responsibility and its share in the guilt. Where this is concerned, on the occasion of the fiftieth anniversary of the *Reichskristallnacht,* the German Bishops Conference was more courageous when it emphasized: ". . . that the Church, which we profess as holy and which we revere as mystery, is also a sinful Church and in need of conversion." For guilt rests not only with individual Christians; since the Middle Ages, Councils have also shared in the guilt by burdening the Jews with many humiliating limitations because of their "unbelief." The discussion group stated clearly that the pagan anti-Semitism of the Nazi regime would not have been possible without the foundation laid by Christian anti-Judaism. The statement also mentioned the role of Pope Pius XII, who as bishop of Rome should have intervened publicly, at least for the Jews of his city, when in 1943, in full view from his windows, they were deported to Auschwitz. Such an action would have been a model for other bishops. The statement also noted critically that after 1945 the Vatican enabled war criminals to flee to the Middle East and Latin America. Here again, John Paul II found the right words when he said in 1994 that the church "instead of offering to the world the witness of a life inspired by the values of faith, indulged in ways of thinking and acting which were truly forms of counter-witness and scandal" (*Tertio millenio adveniente,* § 33).

The beatification of Pius IX in September 2000 was particularly unfortunate. The discussion group wrote a statement in which it pointed out precisely this pope's demonstrable anti-Semitism; in sermons and addresses he let himself be transported in hate-filled tirades against the Jews. In addition, he became notorious when, on July 23, 1858, he had the Jewish child Edgaro Mortara stolen from his parents' house—an atrocity that at the time caused a cry of indignation to be raised all over Europe.

In addition to declarations on fundamental topics and on current events, the discussion group has published two brochures, including one entitled *Journey to the Holy Land* (1998). The other is the booklet *Auschwitz: History and Remembrance* (2002), presented at a press conference in Berlin. This little work can be regarded as fundamental where this topic is concerned.

When, along with these documents, one takes into account the discussion group's intensive work during the German *Katholikentage,* one might conclude that the entire Catholic Church in Germany had undergone a decisive change where the past is concerned. That is certainly true of the German Bishops Conference and the *ZdK.* However, so far it has not been possible to get people at the grassroots level in parishes and schools interested in this important topic. Even though there is nothing to prove that specific anti-Semitism is present there, now as in the past, considerable indifference and great ignorance reign where Judaism is concerned, and this in spite of the fact that Pope John Paul II has again and again emphasized the close links between the church and Judaism.

What are the reasons for this situation? Is it still deep-seated prejudice coming from a long past history? Is it because, for various reasons, the Jewish minority in Germany has little contact with its surroundings? Is it an expression of the general trend of being interested only in current political or church problems?

Whatever the reasons may be, the insight of the past decades is firmly established: Christians have a unique relationship with Jews that is different from their relationship to any other religion. They have the Hebrew Bible in common, the so-called First Testament. Gradually, people have also acknowledged that the Jew Jesus lived and worked in a Jewish world, which meant that in 1938 the great teacher of Judaism, Leo Baeck, could write a book with the title: *Das Evangelium als Urkunde der Jüdischen Glaubensgeschichte (The Gospel as a Document of the History of the Jewish Faith).* Certainly, the theological differences between the two religions must not be blurred if each one's identity is to be upheld, but Catholics must become much more aware of this common foundation than they have been in the past. But we note with gratitude: the ground for a new theological and human awareness is prepared. The discussion group has made an important contribution toward that end. In the future the most important thing will be not to suppress history. Christians must study it thoroughly in order to know whence they have come. Then there is hope that a solid knowledge of Judaism will gain ground in the church and among the faithful.

Through its activities at the *Katholikentage* and its publications, the discussion group has had an important impact above all within Germany. On trips to the United States, Israel, Poland, Hungary, and France it has also reported on its activity and goals in other countries. However, it has become clear that the boundaries for international sharing of information are quite narrow. This is all the more regrettable as the discussion group is the only one in the world in which a country's largest Catholic lay organization has as one of its topics the relationship between Judaism and Christianity in dialogue with Jewish partners. People should reflect on whether and how a similar committee might be created in other countries as well. It would be asking too much of the discussion group itself to take on a European dimension. Such attempts can only be made in the individual countries, and in view of the present-day situation the Catholics have to be the ones to take the first steps toward Jews. It must also be remembered that the discussion group's work is determined by the specific history and situation of Germany, and this cannot simply be transferred to other European countries. It would be pioneering work if, in spite of these problems, the Central Committee succeeded in making the discussion group's work available to a broader European public and could encourage them to take initiatives of their own in this area. That would be an important contribution to the process of European unification.

Theological Issues Outside the Boundaries of the Dialogue?

John T. Pawlikowski

The publications of the discussion group "Jews and Christians" of the Central Committee of German Catholics constitute an invaluable resource for those of us working in Christian-Jewish relations in North America and internationally. They provide challenging, sometimes controversial insights into most of the central issues in the contemporary dialogue. In my brief remarks I would like to focus on a number of the most important ones.

Let me begin with the question of theology in our conversations. These papers are uncompromising in their insistence on the centrality of theology in the dialogue. This is an important assertion that will help those of us here in North America who have held the same conviction but have often had to fight an uphill battle. Because of the significant influence of the great Orthodox Jewish thinker Rabbi Joseph Soloveitchik, theological issues have been regarded as outside the boundaries of the dialogue, even by some who would not fully identify with the Orthodox Jewish perspective. This certainly had been the prevailing view on the Jewish side for years in the conferences sponsored by the National Workshop on Christian-Jewish Relations. It also tended to be the dominant mindset in the official meetings between the Holy See's Commission for Religious Relations with Jews and the International Jewish Commission for Interreligious Consultation.

Some of the resistance to specifically theological dialogue is beginning to erode, but it is still strongly in place in many quarters, especially on the Jewish side. We may in fact see more of it on the Christian side as conservative Catholics enter the conversation. While such Catholics may be open to gaining new spiritual insights as a result of interaction with Jews and their religious tradition, they exhibit the same fear as many Jews that theological exchange could undermine their respective core beliefs. Most of us on the Catholic side who have promoted theological conversations between Jews and Christians have worked under the assumption that in fact some significant theological understandings of our respective faith traditions were inevitable, given the fundamental about-face in Catholic perceptions of Jews and Judaism brought about through Vatican II's rejection of traditional supercessionist theology, an about-face that Gregory Baum has termed the most profound change in the ordinary theological magisterium of the Catholic Church at the Council.

Dabru Emet, the Jewish document on Christianity, has certainly helped create conversation among Jews regarding the role of theology in the Jewish-Christian encounter. While many have rejected some or all of its basic assertions, the document has stimulated a conversation worldwide unlike any we have seen until now. Whether *Dabru Emet* will significantly alter the Jewish-Christian conversation in a lasting way remains an open question. Clearly it is generating the kind of theological reflection the group "Jews and Christians" regards as essential for true contemporary dialogue.

If I were to be critical at all of the approach taken in the German documents it would be to question the insistence that Jews must see themselves as theologically interconnected with Christians. While many Catholic documents, especially the writings of Pope John Paul II, have spoken in this way from the side of Christianity, I would hesitate to make this a precondition for dialogue from the Jewish side. There is such a long tradition of a Christian theology of Jewish covenantal displacement that Jews must be given time to reflect on whether they can authentically include Christianity in some way in their own self-definition. I would hope that Jews do gradually come to this viewpoint, and I have argued in published writings that it will prove increasingly difficult for Christians to maintain their post-Vatican II sense of linkage with Jews at the very level of their basic identity, as Pope John Paul II has put it, unless Jews begin to exhibit some recognition of this reality from their side. But I would not make it as critical a condition for authentic dialogue today as the "Jews and Christians" group would. Such an insistence may also unduly lessen the importance of non-theological issues in the dialogue. Dealing with the Holocaust, with contemporary expressions of anti-Semitism, with historical questions, and with social issues remains central to the dialogue today. Thus making a commitment to theological conversation the ultimate barometer for the authenticity of present-day Catholic-Jewish dialogue may prove to be too narrow a focus and exclude people who have an important non-theological insight to contribute to the reconciliation of our two communities.

*

The German Jewish-Catholic documents, in their unqualified insistence on a critical reappraisal of history, undercut efforts by some to paint an overly rosy picture of the Jewish-Christian relationship over the centuries. The late American pioneer in Catholic-Jewish relations, Fr. Edward Flannery, whose volume *The Anguish of the Jews* remains a classic text on the history of the relationship, once remarked that Jews have memorized the pages of history that Christians have torn out of their books. There is little question that there has existed a deepseated anti-Semitism in popular and theological expressions of Christianity that also found its way into artistic expressions in such places as the cathedral in Strasbourg, France. Unfortunately, we saw a recent revival of such unwillingness to confront history with full honesty in some statements in the 1998 Vatican document on the *Shoah,* "We Remember," where the impression was given that Christians who persecuted Jews did so for reasons that had little to do with official Catholic teaching. Many Catholics regarded the negative portrayal of Judaism on the facade of Strasbourg Cathedral as "authentic" Catholic teaching. And they had every reason to do so.

Such a critical reappraisal of history is certainly called for in terms of church experience during the Holocaust. While I would fully concur with the view that Nazism went well beyond the parameters of classical Christian anti-Semitism and, on the ideological level, was influenced far more by new biological theories than classical anti-Semitism, there is equally little doubt in my mind that classical Christian anti-Semitism was an indispensable factor in the acquiescence and collaboration of many

Christians in the administration of the Nazi program. While German Catholics obviously have faced a special challenge in terms of Auschwitz, all Christians need to wrestle, in partnership with Jews, with its profound theological and moral implications. I for one am grateful that the German documents challenge all so directly and profoundly on this score.

*

Let me conclude my reflections with two additional points. The first has to do with the conversion issue. Jews have raised this question from time to time in the dialogue, especially at those moments when certain evangelical Christian leaders have publicly called for missionary outreach to the Jews. Catholics, on the whole, have tended to sideline the issue. This is certainly true of a number of recent documents on evangelization that have been silent on the issue of converting Jews, neither rejecting it outright nor advocating it.

This approach has worked fairly well until now. Clearly it raises some profound theological issues for Christians regarding the universality of salvation through Christ. But I am not sure the "silent" approach can continue much longer. I said this in an address at a conference at Cambridge University in February 2001. Ultimately the conversion issue tests the depth of change that has or has not taken place in Catholic theology. Recent statements by Cardinal Walter Kasper, who is president of the Holy See's Commission for Religious Relations with Jews, to the effect that Torah suffices for Jewish salvation, and in the Pontifical Biblical Commission document on the Jewish Scriptures and the New Testament, where there is the assertion that Jewish messianic hopes are not in vain, give me some hope that we are moving into a period in which the conversion issue will be discussed far more openly and directly in North America and internationally than has been the case in recent years. I applaud the German documents for putting this question on the table of the dialogue.

*

Finally, I applaud the German documents for raising the issue of "pagan" and "Christian" anti-Semitism. This issue needs further clarification for, as I have said above, too often so-called "pagan anti-Semitism" is used to cover over clear-cut anti-Semitism within the heart of Christianity. Without doubt there is a reality called "pagan anti-Semitism" that reared its ugly head once more in the Nazi era. But it is wrong for Catholics to use "pagan anti-Semitism" as a cover for the reality of Christian anti-Semitism, as has sometimes been the case. It is good that this issue has surfaced in the conversations in Germany.

Overall, then, I found engagement with the German documents a genuine stimulus for my own thinking about central issues in the contemporary Catholic-Jewish dialogue. Clearly these documents show a depth of faith on both sides and an equally strong commitment to work through the most difficult questions as part of the effort to reverse centuries of anti-Semitism and theological anti-Judaism in the churches.

Dialogue out of the Ashes: Jewish-Catholic Dialogue in Germany

Michael A. Signer

"In the place where the wound occurred, healing must begin." This dictum of the Rabbis is central to the documents written by the discussion group Jews and Christians of the *Zentralkomitee der deutschen Katholiken* (Central Committee of German Catholics). Most of the English-speaking audience knows about the world of German Jews from newspapers and journals that have published carefully researched essays monitoring incidents of anti-Semitism such as cemetery desecrations or synagogue bombings. In addition to reports of these incidents there are numerous surveys of the rise or fall of anti-Semitic sentiment. There are also public moments when emotions flare up and Americans hear about a speech in the *Bundestag* that defames the memory of German Jews, or controversies about whether or not a *roman à clef* that describes the death of a Jewish literary critic should be serialized in the news.[1]

For nearly two decades I have come to know another side of post-*Shoah* German life—the engagement of German Lutherans and Catholics with Judaism and their efforts to reach into the horrible abyss created by their parents and grandparents. They have attempted to create what I would call a "dialogue out of the ashes." Since 1985 I have spent every other summer as a lecturer at a week-long summer university on Judaism

1. See Martin Walser's novel, *Tod eines Kritikers* (Frankfurt: Suhrkamp, 2002).

at the *Institut Kirche und Judentum,* sponsored by the Lutheran diocese of Berlin-Brandenburg and organized by Peter von der Osten-Sacken, who directs the institute and holds the chair in New Testament at Humboldt University. Almost two hundred students, Protestant and Catholic, participate in six hours a day of classes focusing on Jews and Judaism. In addition to the summer university, the *EKD* (Evangelical Church in Germany, the institutional form chosen by a community of twenty-four Lutheran, Reformed, and United regional churches) holds meetings and institutes in their academies that focus on a new Christian relationship to Judaism. The Leuenberg Church Fellowship has published a lengthy reflection on the church and Israel (2001) that reflects many years of theological activity.[2] At about the same time I became aware of these activities in the *EKD,* my teacher Jakob J. Petuchowski introduced me at the Sol and Arlene Bronstein Colloquium held at Hebrew Union College in Cincinnati, Ohio, to a group of Catholic theologians that included Clemens Thoma and Hans Hermann Henrix.[3] Both of these scholars spoke of their activity in the discussion group Jews and Christians. An encounter with a wider circle of members, both Catholic and Jewish, of the discussion group occurred in 1989 during the second Sol and Arlene Bronstein Colloquium, held in Augsburg.[4] In the course of that conference I met Hanspeter Heinz, who was responsible for the ongoing organization of the unique group of Catholics and German-speaking Jews. He told me about the work of the discussion group Jews and Christians and its efforts to develop a conversation between these two communities in post-*Shoah* Germany.

2. *Leuenberger Texte/Leuenberg Documents 6: Church and Israel: A Contribution from the Reformation Churches in Europe to the Relationship between Christians and Jews* (Frankfurt: Lembeck, 2001). See also Evanglische Kirche in Deutschland *(EKD), Christen und Juden III: Schritte der Erneuerung im Verhältnis zum Judentum* (Gütersloh: Gütersloher Verlagshaus, 2000). Given the small numbers who ultimately do the work of Jewish-Christian relations in Germany, there is a massive documentation available in Rolf Rendtorff and Hans Hermann Henrix, eds., *Die Kirchen und das Judentum. Dokumente von 1986–2000,* 2 vols., ed. Hans Hermann Henrix and Wolfgang Kraus (Gütersloh: Gütersloher Verlagshaus; Paderborn: Bonifatius 1998, 2001).

3. See Jakob J.Petuchowski, ed., *Defining a Discipline: The Aims and Objectives of Judaeo-Christian Studies* (Cincinnati: Hebrew Union College/Jewish Institute of Religion, 1984).

4. Hanspeter Heinz et al., *Versöhnung in der jüdischen und christlichen Liturgie,* QD 124 (Freiburg, Basel, and Vienna: Herder, 1990).

*

The documents in this volume indicate the group's attempts to create an awareness of the developments in Catholic theology after the Second Vatican Council. However, the search for Jewish "partners" in the discussion was very difficult. The community of Jews in Germany that had given birth to the rich culture of authors such as Martin Buber, Franz Rosenzweig, and Rabbi Leo Baeck had been utterly destroyed. The community of Jews who did live in postwar Germany were, in the majority, refugees from the concentration camps who thought of themselves as preparing for emigration rather than permanent settlement. In the immediate postwar years Jews of German cultural background lived either in America or England, and their return to any "conversation" in Germany that was grounded in a religious environment took time to evolve. However, the first courageous steps by Jews to join this conversation were taken by Ernst Ludwig Ehrlich and Rabbi Marcel Marcus in Switzerland, as well as Rabbi Nathan Peter Levinson and Edna Brocke in Germany.[5] Their participation was based both on a profound hope for new directions in the relationships between Jews and the Catholic Church and on a deep suspicion about whether trust could really be established. In parallel to the experience of the Jewish-Catholic dialogue in America, their initial direction seems to have been to help their Catholic colleagues understand the deep connection between modern anti-Semitism and the Christian teachings of contempt that had been at its foundation.

The approach of the German discussion group to Jewish-Catholic relations was built on two foundations: theological reflection and experience. In the spirit of Vatican Council II, which called for special attention to the "signs of the times," this group set off on a bold course that permitted experience and theological reflection to be in dialogue with one another rather than in a hierarchy that places speculative thought above experience. As any reader of the essays in this volume can easily observe, they reflect a balance between lived experiences and thought, which allows them to reach creative insights that can enrich the growing literature of Jewish-Christian dialogue.

5. Marcel Marcus, Ekkehard W. Stegemann, and Erich Zenger, eds., *Israel und Kirche heute: Beiträge zum christlich-jüdischen Gespräch für Ernst Ludwig Ehrlich* (Freiburg, Basel, and Vienna: Herder, 1991), and Julius H. Schoeps, ed., *Aus zweier Zeugen Mund: Festschrift für Pnina Nave Levinson und Peter Nathan Levinson* (Gerlingen: Bleicher Verlag, 1992).

The 1979 working paper on "Theological Issues for Jewish-Christian Dialogue" demonstrates this balance of experience and theological reflection. Both Jews and Christians enter into a relationship in the common hope that they may work for the complete fulfillment of the reign of God. This new relationship derives from the revelation in Scripture that the God of Israel has acted in human history. This divine action is sustained by human responsibility to work toward this establishment that Jews call *Tikkun ʿOlam* (the repair of the world). The connection between the search for understanding of God in history and the human responsibility imposed on Jews and Christians obliges these two peoples—each with its unique understanding of that revelation—to join in dialogue. This document underlines the importance of mutual understanding. It emphasizes that the Jewish people is not a historical relic that continues in the world only as a result of their witness to the Hebrew Bible. Christians will come to understand the role of Jews *post-Christum* as they oblige themselves to be in conversation and companionship with Jews as a continuous and living tradition. Similarly, Jews will only learn about the profound Christian yearning to create what Augustine called "a civilization based on love" as a result of listening to the religious dimensions of their self-explanation. Clearly, this type of dialogue will require mutual respect and a great deal of patience and the freedom to ask embarrassing questions of one another. The document "Theological Issues for Jewish-Christian Dialogue" created both the foundation of a continuing conversation and the framework for a healthy dialogue that permitted these questions to be raised, and answers to emerge.

*

From the earliest years of the group it was clear to them that the absence of a vital Jewish community in Germany would oblige them to travel outside their own country in order to discover what was happening in other communities. Their first journey was to Israel, the newest center of Jewish life in 1975. This was followed by study-tours to New York (1986), Hungary (1991), Poland (1993), and Paris (1999). The only evidence of these study-tours in the current volume is "A Journey to the Holy Land," first published in 1974 and revised in 1984 and again in 1998. One cannot fail to be impressed with the quality of the observations and the sincere effort to understand how Jews, Christians, and Muslims struggled to find coexistence in a land considered sacred to each of their religions. It is possible to read this document as a meditative preparation for German Catholics visiting the state of Israel. The reader is prepared for both the enthusiastic expectations of a journey of pilgrimage and the reality of life in the land itself. Each religious community is described sympathetically.

It is particularly noteworthy that the continuity of Jewish longing for the land of Israel and the permanence of actual Jews living there are highlighted. The descriptions of the *Shoah* and the plural forms of Jewish life in Israel would be very helpful to any Christian traveler there. The element of Jewish-Christian dialogue also enters the document in the description of Christian communities in Israel. They will find "evidence of their own history in the Holy Land, a history no longer related to Judaism." Christians are warned that "the Holy Land should not be regarded as a museum. A visit there should not only be a nostalgic look at the past but also an opportunity to perceive [its] diversity, richness, and difficulties." The discussion of "problems" is particularly impressive. The discussion group's document does not jump to easy resolutions or self-righteous denunciations of power used by the Israelis. The participants do not appeal to the cliché used by many Christians that Jews come to dialogue with Christians only for the sake of politics. Traveling together through Israel and other lands has permitted this discussion group the time to develop a level of genuine knowledge of the Other. One can only imagine the hours of discussion by Jews and Christians in this group that yielded the following sober assessment of the relationship between Judaism as a religion and the so-called "political" dimension of the Jewish people: "The history of the Jewish people in the nineteenth and twentieth centuries shows how religious tradition, under certain circumstances, is driven by necessity to play a political role in history. Whether or not Christian visitors approve of the state of affairs in the country today, the mere existence of the state of Israel confronts them with the necessity to recognize that a faith that has provided a minority the means to survive without state or political protection can and must continuously be associated with matters of state and politics." These sentences, together with the concluding sections of this remarkable paper, will surely provide participants in Jewish-Christian dialogue in English-speaking countries with material for reflection.

*

Another dimension of the extraordinary honesty that developed within the discussion group is revealed in their 1988 document, "After Fifty Years: How Can We Talk about Guilt, Suffering, and Reconciliation?" Both the message of the document and the process that led to the final version reveal the tensions that remain between Jews and Christians when the neuralgic pressure point of the *Shoah* is raised. The horror of the *Reichskristallnacht* (9 November 1938) is a flashpoint every year in Germany. As each subsequent generation comes to terms with the horror of the Nazi past there is a longing to draw a line under it and move forward. However, the notion of *extinctio memoriae* is impossible for Christians and Jews.[6] My Christian students at the University of Notre Dame attend my courses with the same eager question: "How was it possible for baptized Christians to perpetrate such atrocities against Jews? How could followers of Jesus have participated in violent acts that almost led to the extinction of the Jewish people?" Their deepest anxiety derives from the question they all ask themselves: "What would I have done if I had been there at that time?" The discussion group's document provides them with both a message and a method. The fundamental message is that guilt can be expiated by *Teshuvah* (repentance), and that ultimately forgiveness is far less important than undertaking a process of critical self-examination and, with the clarity that emerges from the examination, arriving at a personal commitment to avoid the behavior that led to the sin. However, this document also demonstrates that the most effective method for Jewish-Christian dialogue is the study of the texts of our tradition. The arguments over the nature of guilt and expiation began when the Jewish members of the group proposed the study of Maimonides' *Hilchot T'shuvah* (Laws of Repentance). As Jews and Christians studied a twelfth-century Jewish philosopher and legal scholar together, the Christians began to recognize a profound similarity to the Rite of Reconciliation. Although these processes are not identical, there were sufficient points

6. See the interesting reflections of Hanspeter Heinz, "The Celebration of the Sacraments and the Teaching of the Commandments in the Age of Religious Consumerism, or History and Memory in Christian Communities Since the Second Vatican Council," in Michael A. Signer, ed., *Memory and History in Christianity and Judaism* (Notre Dame: University of Notre Dame Press, 2000) 145–69, and the response by David Ellenson, "History, Memory, and Relationship" on pp. 170–81 of the same volume.

of contact to permit an exchange of ideas between two religious communities. A common language emerged that respected the unique demands of each tradition. Neither religious community was forced to adopt the position held by the other, but the process of study permitted each side to develop a document that was authentic and not apologetic. It is precisely this engagement that sets the foundation of trust that is the *conditio sine qua non* for dialogue between two religious traditions that have been alienated from one another for two millennia.[7]

*

The other documents in this collection reveal the discussion group and its work as an advisory commission to the Central Committee of German Catholics and as a help to the German Bishops Conference. Position papers on the *Catechism of the Catholic Church,* the convent at Auschwitz, the canonization of Edith Stein or Pius IX, and on "We Remember," the document of the Vatican Commission on Religious Relations with the Jews on the *Shoah,* have their analogues in documents written in the United States by the local priest/rabbi dialogue in Los Angeles produced in the 1970s and 1980s, and more recently on the national level by the National Council of Synagogues and the United States Conference of Catholic Bishops Commission on Religious Relations with the Jewish People. With each intervention the discussion group reflects the same intellectual intensity and theological acumen. They reveal that the exchange between Christians and Jews produces a very different interpretation of events than when Christians gather by themselves to write about Jews and Judaism. Speaking and writing with the faces of the other religious community present produces unique and sometimes bold formulations. The attempt to speak and write together may be the path toward what Pope John Paul II has urged throughout his papacy: that these two communities become a "blessing to one another and then a blessing to the world."

I hope that the English-speaking public gains an appreciation of the difficulties faced by the discussion group of the Central Committee of

7. I suggested the reading of religious texts in the presence of one another as the fundamental basis for Jewish-Christian dialogue in my article, "*Speculum Concilii:* Through the Mirror Brightly," in Roger Brooks, ed., *Unanswered Questions: Theological Views of Jewish-Christian Relations* (Notre Dame: University of Notre Dame Press, 1988) 105–27.

German Catholics in creating these documents. The Catholic discussion partners have reached out to members of a Jewish community in Germany that is still on the way to finding its own identity. The dialogue in Germany that is reflected in these pages derives from conversations between Jews and Catholics who spoke in the German language after the *Shoah*. Perhaps in their efforts we can see the perils and the opportunities of creating a new language that both respects the past and is courageous enough to move into an uncertain but hopeful future.

From Contempt to Respect for Jews

Martin Stoehr

All who collaborate in the renewal of the relationship between Jews and Christians know that these efforts are really just beginning. In all the churches the venom of anti-Jewish ways of thinking has had too deep an effect through teaching, catechesis, and preaching, even if the teaching traditions and the forms of piety are very different from one church to the other. Indifference in these matters prolongs the life of anti-Jewish prejudice. It is not possible to examine critically and formulate anew what was taught against the Jewish people or thought and published without regard to them for almost two thousand years. Only a minority of people is working creatively on these issues.

I have known many members of the discussion group "Jews and Christians" of the Central Committee of German Catholics through welcome occasions for cooperation, and I have studied their statements. As a Protestant theologian who is committed to the same task, I have rejoiced since coming in contact with these documents, because there are many points of agreement. Together with many others I am aghast over the fact that it is the *Shoah* and not the Christian message which gave the first decisive impetus toward a new orientation. Cain tries to dialogue after Abel has been murdered.

*

The misconception that the renewal of Christian-Jewish relations is a specific theological issue and thus of interest only to a few indispensable specialists is still widespread. But the matter at hand is no less and no more than the fundamental understanding of church and theology. Do we see our relationship to the Jewish people as only historical, something that must be studied so as to come to a better understanding of the prehistory of Christianity? Or do we take seriously the fact that Jesus was a Jew and that he did not leave his Jewish community? The usual thesis, according to which Jesus' critical position in discussions with the Pharisees and scribes reflects his "original words," and that claims that Jesus "breaks open the limits of the Torah and particularism," testifies to a lack of knowledge of the Jewish culture of discussion. It is precisely critical and "risky" interpretations that take the tradition seriously by bringing it into the present. And that kind of discussion is never without conflict.

Jews and Christians adore the same God, the God who created the world, who through his revelation lets this world know him, his actions, and his word, who graciously and critically accompanies this world, who renews and redeems it. This God called Israel to be his witness in the midst of the nations. Do Christians know that they received their knowledge of God through Israel, where God was born, and that they only receive this knowledge properly if they see in Israel not only their living mother, but also their sister? In Israel the mother and the sister are living with the church now, in the present time, until God will be all in all and Israel will be saved.

The church and Israel read the same Sacred Scripture. For Israel, this is the Bible; for the churches, it is the largest part of the Bible and has equal rights with the New Testament. Jews and Christians read this Sacred Scripture differently in some parts, as their various traditions show: on the one hand, the oral revelation in Talmud and Midrash, on the other, the revelation of Jesus in the New Testament and the subsequent traditions of the church fathers, the councils, synods, and creeds.

The fact that the Old Testament, which is not at all obsolete (the Hebrew Bible, Tanakh, the First Testament) is read differently by Jews and Christians is no reason for separation. The same is true of both Jewish and Christian ways of interpreting the Bible. But this reality does give us the decisive reason for deepening our communication and solidarity. For God's sake and that of humanity, no voice that tries to understand the Word of God for human beings and situations today may be muted. Those who drink from the same source communicate at that source and about that source; they speak about how this living stream can be brought not only to their own needs, but also how the living water of God's justice and righteousness, of God's truth and love, God's peace and spirit can be for the good of human beings, for whom the Eternal has determined it.

It is not easy to endure in what we have in common and in our differences, in identity and openness. Paul talks about that in his letter to Rome, above all in chapters 9–11. There, we find no immutable decisions valid for all eternity. Full of hope, Paul struggles with the task of showing the community in Rome, which is apparently already dominated by Gentile Christians, that Israel is not rejected, but remains God's chosen child. At the same time Paul goes beyond his earlier statement (1 Thess 2:13-16) linking pre-Christian contempt for Jews with the specifically Christian argument of "deicide." This text affected history in an anti-Jewish way, as did John 8:44—and John 4:22 ("Salvation is from the Jews") did not have such a historic effect. For centuries the church fought against accepting the positive role for Israel that is to be found in the New Testament. Today there is ecumenical agreement in emphasizing more what is common to the two stories in the continuity of the Hebrew Bible without playing down the differences.

In view of the One and Eternal's will to save the world (with Israel!), Christian feelings of superiority are pagan arrogance. All too often Christians believed they could pass judgment on the Jews as at the Last Judgment. All too often such thinking and such practice had negative, even fatal consequences for the Jews. Christianity should be glad that God's truth stands "on the testimony of two witnesses" (Deut 19:15; Matt 18:16; 2 Cor 13:1; 1 Tim 5:19). Among the nations the church praises the God of Israel, not just any god. And as Christians believe, to praise is to live. This foundation and this goal determine the path of the churches: "Rejoice, you nations, you *Goyim*, with God's people" (Deut 32:43 and Rom 15:9). We have set out on this path together, but nowhere near everyone has done so. In no way are we already at the end of this journey. In no way has it been sufficiently implemented in books for university study, in school books, sermons, and pastoral care.

*

In everyday life, religiously formed prejudices concerning the Jewish people continue. Things that were once said and thought against the Jews in a Christian context continue to work in the secular context. Even in the media and politics we can hear talk about the "Old Testament God of revenge," "Pharisaic hypocrisy," "Jewish avarice," and the "treacherous tendency" that can be illustrated with "Judas," the "Jewish prototype," and so on. To renew relations between Jews and Christians means not only enlightening people within our own Christian ranks; it also requires that we be attentive within a secularized society that was shaped by Christianity. Theology is never without consequences, either in its "false" statements or in the "true" ones. "Pagan" anti-Semitism can be as fatal for the Jewish minority as Semitic religious hatred of the Jews. Both types of contempt for Jews belong within the churches' area of responsibility. What characterizes the documents contained in this volume is that they read and understand the Bible in a new way, with the eyes of Jesus and of their Jewish authors. The history of Jews and Christians is marked by a profound asymmetry: on the one side we have Christianity, which often exercised power (in many forms) and represented the majority. For a long time the result was that Christianity described its own position by negating Judaism. Now it has to learn to find its own self-understanding without the concept of an enemy and a dark backdrop. That includes acknowledging and taking seriously the self-understandings of a multifaceted Judaism. The discussion group "Jews and Christians," like other similar commissions, speaks *with* Jews and not *about* them. Learning face to face with Israel leads to abandoning a Christian monopoly in interpreting the biblical message, something too often taken for granted. This message is richer than inner-Christian and inner-theological discourse assume.

On the other side there is the minority of the Jewish people. In the Diaspora and in the state of Israel it is struggling for equal rights and for a place in the world of the nations. In some societies this Jewish minority is experiencing latent or open discrimination to this day. Anti-Semitism is by no means dead. Both in authoritarian societies and in democratic ones there is a sediment of anti-Semitism. It appears in many camouflages, including anti-Zionism. In the state of Israel the Jewish people as a majority is still struggling for its right to live, and for a just and peaceful life together with the Palestinian people.

The document initiated by rabbis and professors from the United States, *Dabru Emet* (Speak Truth), speaks of the fact that there has been an unprecedented shift in Jewish and Christian relations in recent years. This magnificent response to the beginning of a Christian process of renewal is an encouragement not to grow slack but rather to continue working. Old and new thinking is alive and active in an asynchronic side-by-side process in Christian congregations as well as in theological faculties.

*

The texts published here, which speak of a renewal in thinking and acting, were written by the group within German Catholicism that has pushed the learning process for renewal forward most consistently. This process took place and is taking place in a country where, even now, only a small number of Jews live, though their number is growing fast. The churches have to face the question of why "dialogue" is coming too late, after the murder of six million Jews in Europe. For me it is and remains humbling and at the same time encouraging to have heard the answer of a rabbi who returned to Germany after 1945. For him, the reason why it was possible to live in the land of the murderers and of those who looked away, and to work together with Christians, was: "Because there was an Alfred Delp here and a Dietrich Bonhoeffer." One of the most profound impressions for those involved in dialogue is the fact that there were and are Jewish partners in dialogue who—in spite of all that happened—are willing to help the churches and Christians to begin anew. This dialogue is no small talk. For the most part the work done is critical and self-critical enlightenment on false directions taken by the churches both in their thinking and in their practice. That is the only means possible for Jews and Christians to find the way into a better future.

*

No new beginning is possible without a recognition and confession of guilt. That is a common conviction in all Christian statements since 1945. After the monstrosity of the mass murder, it was and is a matter of recognizing, naming, and confessing the guilt. What happened, why so many people from all social milieus could become accomplices with evil, why resistance was so weak, must be clearly analyzed and expressed insofar as it is at all possible to explain the *Shoah*. Although there was (and is) anti-Semitism and religious anti-Judaism in many countries and cultures, it was only in Germany that the hatred turned into mass murder. What specific German conditions can be named for that? All the social institutions in this country—the courts, administration, trains, media, schools, universities, industry, army, culture, even the churches—deserted people of Jewish origin. We must not forget the few brave exceptions. But all the institutions and structures that, according to both Jewish and Christian understanding, "exist for people," (knowingly or in an opportunistic way) did not work for "the weakest and most defenseless brothers of Jesus Christ," but rather for the strong, the armed power. That is the only way an unprecedented industrial death machinery could be prepared and put to work.

Such precise acknowledging, naming, and confessing must be done not only before God, but also before people, publicly, above all before the victims and the survivors. In this, the intention is not to obtain forgiveness from the victims. Who could speak from among the dead and for the dead? Dietrich Bonhoeffer, in his *Ethics,* written contrary to law and left unfinished at his death, wrote to his church (that is, the little Confessing Church) as early as 1941: "The only way to turn back is through recognition of the guilt."[1] Because the church understands itself to be the living Body of Christ it betrayed what it is, that is, Christ himself. Bonhoeffer reveals the guilt clearly when he speaks of all the Ten Commandments of the Decalogue and then writes concerning the Jews: "The Church confesses that she has witnessed the lawless application of brutal force, the physical and spiritual suffering of countless innocent people, oppression, hatred and murder, and that she has not raised her voice on behalf of the victims and has not found ways to hasten to their aid. She is guilty of the death of the weakest and most defenseless brothers of Jesus Christ."[2] In the same context—and surely uniquely in the Protestant theology of his time—he pointed out: "Western history is, by God's will, indissolubly linked with the people of Israel, not only genetically but also in a genuine uninterrupted encounter. The Jews keep open the question of Christ."[3]

*

In February 1946, in the name of Christianity, the Ecumenical Council of Churches in Geneva, which was still in its formative stages, penitently

1. Dietrich Bonhoeffer, *Ethics,* ed. Eberhard Bethge, tr. Neville Horton Smith (London and Glasgow: Collins/Fontana Books, 1964) 110.

2. Ibid. 114.

3. Ibid.

confessed the churches' failure and at the same time spoke out against every form of anti-Semitism and in favor of all efforts at finding new homelands for the survivors. At its official foundation in 1948 it emphasized the abiding election of Israel and Christianity's Jewish heritage. With regard to the state of Israel, which it recognized from its very beginning, it said that the churches are in duty bound to pray and work for an order in Palestine as just as may be in the midst of our human disorder.[4] However, at the time the obligation to evangelize was added, also where the Jews were concerned. In matters concerning the mission to the Jews, the "christological question, that is to say the question concerning the Messiah," was not "left open" in 1948. A feeling of superiority was still very much alive. The "openness of the christological question" does not demand that the churches renounce or relativize their confession of faith in Christ. They only have to take seriously what is contained in their doctrine: In the end, it is God who will judge concerning faith in the Messiah in both of his children. For there is fundamental biblical agreement that Israel, like the church—or better: the church, like Israel—believes in and prays for the coming of the messianic kingdom, even if the future of the one who is to come (again) varies according to the living colors of hope. Texts like Matthew 7:21 and 25:31-46 strengthen the reliability *(certitudo)* of Christian faith, but not its security *(securitas)*. A person's certainty in his or her own faith is no obstacle to dialogue, but the security that turns the other into an object is. Such an understanding has consequences: The Synod of the Reformed Church in the Netherlands declared for the first time in 1951 in its Church Order that, because of the relationship Church—Israel, the decisive element was dialogue, whereas for work among the nations it was mission.[5] In 1980 the Synod of the Church of the Rhineland, in an official decision, rejected the mission to the Jews.[6]

The connection between the confession of guilt and the profession of faith in the abiding election of Israel is clear: The crux of the erroneous development in the church's teaching and practice was and is the convic-

4. Both texts can be found in German in Rolf Rendtorff and Hans Hermann Henrix, eds., *Die Kirchen und das Judentum. Dokumente von 1945–1985* (Paderborn: Gütersloh, 1988) 324–29; in English, cf. www.jcrelations.net/index.htm under Statements. Ecumenical Statements. Documents of the World Council of Churches. First Assembly in Amsterdam, 1948.

5. Rendtorff and Henrix, eds., *Die Kirchen und das Judentum*, 447.

6. Ibid. 593–96; in English, cf. www.jcrelations.net/index.htm, Statements. Ecumenical Statements.

tion that, after the appearance of Jesus Christ and his confirmation through God in the resurrection and in the founding of the church on Pentecost, the church is the true Israel. The real Israel is then nothing but the precursor from whom the church inherited and whom the church disinherited, so that it is now dismissed and rejected by God in its vocation to bear witness.

This brings us to the decisive question: What should be the self-understanding of a church that is "taken into God's covenant with Israel, that shares in God's covenant, that, like Israel, is on the way toward God's kingdom that is to come," as is said in the various church resolutions? How does such a church profess its faith in Jesus, the Messiah, without ignoring the biblically founded Jewish question as to the visibility and public manifestation of the redemption of Israel and the world? Has not every Christian statement that pushes Israel into a deficit position in relationship to Christianity become impossible? Do not both lag behind that to which God has called them? Is the church not the preparation for the Messiah, as Maimonides put it, *praeparatio messianica* and not *perfectio messianica,* messianic fulfillment? Is not this the great task that the church (and Islam!) have, to make known God's Name and Word to the furthest islands, as Maimonides said in recognition of them both? Is it not part of the practice, the prayer, and the teaching of the church to be on the way in hope and in action? As in the Bible's law concerning witnesses, and as in the sending forth of the disciples of Jesus, is it not helpful to be on the way in groups of two? The ecclesiological and christological questions I have consciously raised show which tasks await a church that is willing to dialogue while listening both to Scripture and to Israel.

*

It would be a misunderstanding if we thought the renewal process in relations between Jews and Christians were only about teaching, catechesis, and preaching. It is also and first of all the task of a renewal in praxis. It was in its praxis that the church failed in its solidarity with Jews. Being Jesus' disciples had not kept up with christology. When I read the documents presented here and those coming from other churches, it becomes wonderfully clear that here, too, new paths are being broken. Being disciples of Christ does not mean that a Christian theory is implemented in a Christian praxis. Amazingly, for Israel, doing the will of God is the first answer to God's revelation: "All that the Lord has spoken we will do" (Exod 24:7). The New Testament is no different.

Against this background, the fact that many declarations speak of a common responsibility is consistent. God has made his people and his church to be active witnesses of God's Torah. And this teaching for life—the word "Law" translates "Torah" in much too narrow a sense—consists in what God is, what God does, and what God says. God shares his justice and his love, his truth and his peace, his freedom and his trust with his creatures. The religions have to do what honest scholarly work cannot do, what practical politics may not do, that is, determine what these great words mean in terms of everyday values. The religions have the responsibility of helping people in scholarly work and politics, in education, and those coping with life, experience what is a just and merciful life, how truth and peace are practiced, how liberation (from guilt, misery, or violence) and trust become reality. They communicate with the questions concerning people's personal lives and world society, of which they are a part. Human success in human living, in living together, and in surviving is on God's agenda. And God's agenda is the word for the life of Israel and the church.

Members of the Discussion Group "Jews and Christians" of the Central Committee of German Catholics

Appendix A

Chairman: Prof. Dr. Hanspeter Heinz
Director: Dr. Detlef Stäps, *Ecclesiastical Rector, Central Committee of German Catholics*

Daniel Alter
Rabbinic Student, Berlin

Prof. Dr. Reinhold Bohlen
Rector, Theological Department, Trier, and Professor of Introduction to Biblical Studies

Dr. Henry G. Brandt
Rabbi for Westphalia, Dortmund

Prof. Dr. Wilhelm Breuning
Professor Emeritus of Dogmatics, University of Bonn

Prof. Dr. Micha Brumlik
Professor of Pedagogy, University of Frankfurt; Director, Fritz-Bauer-Institute, Frankfurt.

Dr. Edna Brocke
Director, The Old Synagogue Memorial, Essen, and Teacher of Religious Education, Jewish Community, Krefeld.

Prof. Dr. Christoph Dohmen
Professor of Old Testament Studies, University of Regensburg

Prof. Dr. Ernst Ludwig Ehrlich
Honorary Professor of Modern Jewish History and Literature, University of Bern; European Director of B'nai Brith

Prof. Dr. Hubert Frankemoelle
Professor of New Testament Studies, University of Paderborn

Dr. Wilfried Hagemann
Director of the Catholic Seminary, Diocese of Muenster

Prof. Dr. Hanspeter Heinz
Professor of Pastoral Theology, University of Augsburg

Dr. Hans Hermann Henrix
Director, Episcopal Education Center, Diocese of Aachen

Dr. Walter Homolka
Executive Director, Abraham Geiger College, University of Potsdam

Prof. Dr. Herbert Immenkoetter
Professor of Medieval and Modern Church History, University of Augsburg

Ruth Kahana-Geyer
Teacher of Religious Education, Jewish Community, Bonn

Dr. Uri Kaufmann
Teacher and Researcher on Central European Jewish History, Heidelberg

Prof. Dr. Klaus Kienzler
Professor of Fundamental Theology, University of Augsburg

Dr. Ansgar Koschel
Director, Episcopal Education Center "Rhabanus Maurus," Diocese of Limburg

Petra Kunik
Writer, Frankfurt am Main

Prof. Dr. Verena Lenzen
Professor of Judaic Studies, Theology, and Christian-Jewish Dialogue, and Director, Institute for Jewish-Christian Research, University of Luzern

Dagmar Mensink
Manager of Religious Affairs for the Executive Committee of the German Social Democratic Party (SPD)

Ellen Presser
Biologist and Director of the Center of Youth and Culture, Israeli Community, Munich

Prof. Michael A. Signer
Abrams Professor of Jewish Thought and Culture, Department of Theology, University of Notre Dame, South Bend, Indiana

Dr. Herman Simon
Director, Centrum Judaicum, Berlin

Werner Trutwin
Retired Headmaster, Heinrich-Hertz-Gymnasium, Bonn

Rita Waschbüsch
Former President, Central Committee of German Catholics

Prof. Dr. Josef Wohlmuth
Professor Emeritus of Dogmatics, University of Bonn

Prof. Dr. Erich Zenger
Professor Emeritus of Old Testament Studies, University of Münster

Publications of the Discussion Group "Jews and Christians"

Appendix B

1. Statements

"Theologische Schwerpunkte des jüdisch-christlichen Gesprächs." Working paper, 8 May 1979: In Zentralkomitee der deutschen Katholiken, Bonn, *Berichte und Dokumente* 39 (1979) 6–19; also in Rolf Rendtorff and Hans Hermann Henrix, eds., *Die Kirchen und das Judentum. Dokumente von 1945–1985,* 3d ed. Paderborn: Bonifatius; Gütersloh: Gütersloher Verlagshaus, 2001, 252–62.

English: "Important Theological Issues for Jewish-Christian Dialogue." Working paper, 8 May 1979: In Central Committee of German Catholics, Bonn, *Reports and Documents* 39 (1979) 6–19. Translation: Colleen Wunsch, Augsburg.

"Merksätze und Leitlinien für eine Reise ins Heilige Land," ed. Zentralkomitee der deutschen Katholiken und Katholisches Bibelwerk. Stuttgart: Katholisches Bibelwerk, 1974 ; rev. ed. "Reise ins Heilige Land," (1984); also in Rendtorff and Henrix, eds., *Die Kirchen und das Judentum* (2001, 288–303). Revised and expanded ed. Stuttgart: Katholisches Bibelwerk, 1998.

English: "Guidelines for a Journey to the Holy Land," published by the Central Committee of German Catholics and the Catholic Bible Institute. Stuttgart: Catholic Bible Institute, 1974; rev. ed. "A Journey to the Holy Land" (1984). Translation: Helga Sourek, Köln, and Colleen Wunsch, Augsburg.

"Nach 50 Jahren—wie reden von Schuld, Leid und Versoehnung?" Declaration, 6 January 1988, in: *Berichte und Dokumente* 68 (1988) 16–46; also in Hans Hermann Henrix and Wolfgang Kraus, eds., *Die Kirchen und das Judentum. Dokumente von*

1986–2000. Paderborn: Bonifatius; Gütersloh: Gütersloher Verlagshaus, 2001, 341–53; also available as an offprint with an introduction by Hanspeter Heinz und Rabbi Marcel Marcus and a summary of the discussions in the assembly of the Zentralkomitee der deutschen Katholiken.

English: "After Fifty Years: How Can We Talk about Guilt, Suffering, and Reconciliation?" Declaration, 6 January 1988, in: *Reports and Documents* 68 (1988) 16–46. Translation: Sr. Dr. Katherine Wolff, Jerusalem, and Colleen Wunsch, Augsburg.

"Kloster und Kreuz in Auschwitz?" Declaration, 4 April 1990, in: *Berichte und Dokumente* 75 (1990) 45–52; also in Henrix and Kraus eds., *Die Kirchen und das Judentum* (2001) 374–78.

English: "Convent and Cross in Auschwitz?" Declaration, 4 April 1990. Translation: Sr. Dr. Katherine Wolff, Jerusalem, and Colleen Wunsch, Augsburg.

"Juden und Judentum im neuen Katechismus der Katholischen Kirche—Ein Zwischenruf." Discussion paper, 29 January 1996, in: *Berichte und Dokumente* 101 (1996) 27–31; also in Henrix and Kraus, eds., *Die Kirchen und das Judentum* (2001) 387–91; also available as an offprint, with supplementary remarks by Eugene J. Fisher, James L. Heft, Alan Mittleman, and Michael A. Signer.

English: "Jews and Judaism in the New Catechism of the Catholic Church—an Intervention." Also available as an offprint, with supplementary remarks by Eugene J. Fisher, James L. Heft, Alan Mittleman, and Michael A. Signer. Translation: Thomas Norris, Maynooth, Ireland, and Hanspeter Heinz, Augsburg.

"Nachdenken über die *Schoa*. Mitschuld und Verantwortung der katholischen Kirche. Zur Erklärung der Vatikanischen Kommission für die religiösen Beziehungen zu den Juden vom 16. März 1998." Position paper, 4 September 1998, in: *Berichte und Dokumente* 109 (1999) 77–85; also in Henrix and Kraus, eds., *Die Kirchen und das Judentum* (2001) 392–99.

English: "Reflections on the *Shoah*. The Catholic Church's Share of the Blame and Responsibility: A Statement Concerning the Declaration of the Vatican Commission for Religious Relationships with the Jews of March 16, 1998." Position paper, 4 September 1988, in: *Reports and Documents* 109 (1999) 77–85. Translation: Martha Matesich, Münster, and Colleen Wunsch, Augsburg.

"Papst Pius IX. und die Juden." Position paper, 21 July 2000, in: *Berichte und Dokumente* 113 (2001) 51–53.

English: "Pope Pius IX. and the Jews." Position paper, 21 July 2000, in: *Reports and Documents* 113 (2001) 51–53.

"Auschwitz—Geschichte und Gedenken," ed. Zentralkomitee der deutschen Katholiken und Katholisches Bibelwerk. Stuttgart: Katholisches Bibelwerk, 2002.

English: "Auschwitz: History and Remembrance," published by the Central Committee of German Catholics and Catholic Bible Institute. Stuttgart: Catholic Bible Institute, 2002.

"Juden und Christen in Deutschland: Verantwortete Zeitgenossenschaft in einer pluralen Gessellschaft." A Declaration, 13 April 2005, in Zentralkomitee der deutschen Katholiken, Bonn, *Berichte und Dokumente* (2005) 209–234.

English: "Jews and Christians in Germany: Responsibility in Today's Pluralistic Society." Translation: Claus Jungkunz and Michael A. Signer.

2. Documentations of Conferences and Trips

(published in German only)

Wilhelm Breuning and Nathan Peter Levinson. *Zeugnis und Rechenschaft. Ein christlich-jüdisches Gespräch*. Stuttgart: Katholisches Bibelwerk, 1982.

[Wilhelm Breuning and Nathan Peter Levinson. *Witness and Dialogue. A Christian-Jewish Discussion.*]

Wilhelm Breuning and Hanspeter Heinz, eds. *Damit die Erde menschlich bleibt. Gemeinsame Verantwortung von Juden und Christen für die Zukunft.* Freiburg, Basel, and Vienna: Herder, 1985.

[Wilhelm Breuning and Hanspeter Heinz, eds. *That the Earth May Remain Human: Mutual Responsibility of Jews and Christians for the Future.*]

"Dokumentation der Studienreise von Präsidium und Gesprächskreis 'Juden und Christen' des Zentralkomitees der deutschen Katholiken vom 8.-16. März 1986 nach New York und Washington," in: *Berichte und Dokumente* 63 (1987) 1–66.

["Report of a study tour by the executive committee of the Central Committee of German Catholics and the discussion group 'Jews and Christians,' to New York and Washington, March 8-16, 1986," in: *Reports and Documents* 63 (1987) 1–66.]

"Bericht über eine Reise des Präsidiums des Zentralkomitees der deutschen Katholiken und von Mitgliedern des Gesprächskreises 'Juden und Christen' nach Ungarn vom 5. bis 10. April 1991," in: *Berichte und Dokumente* 80 (1991) 1–32.

["Report of a study tour by the executive committee of the Central Committee of German Catholics and the discussion group 'Jews and Christians' to Hungary, April 5–10, 1991," in: *Reports and Documents* 80 (1991) 1–32.]

"Bericht über die Polenreise des Präsidiums des Zentralkomitees der deutschen Katholiken und des Gesprächskreises 'Juden und Christen' vom 10. bis 17. Oktober 1993," in: *Berichte und Dokumente* 92 (1994) 1–107.

["Report of a study tour by the executive committee of the Central Committee of German Catholics and the discussion group 'Jews and Christians' to Poland, October 10–17, 1993," in: *Reports and Documents* 92 (1994) 1–107.]

"Die Gottrede von Juden und Christen unter den Herausförderungen der säkularen Welt. Symposion am 22./23. November 1995 in der Katholischen Akademie Berlin," in: *Berichte und Dokumente* 103 (1996) 1–95; also available as Dieter Henrich, Johann Baptist Metz, Bernd Jochen Hilberath, and Zwi Werblowsky, *Die Gottrede von Juden und Christen unter den Herausforderungen der säkularen*

Welt. Symposion am 22./23. November 1995 in der Katholischen Akademie Berlin. Münster: Lit-Verlag, 1997.

["How Can Jews and Christians Speak about God in the Modern Secular World? Symposium November 22–23, 1995 in the Episcopal Education Center of the Diocese of Berlin," also available as Dieter Henrich, Johann Baptist Metz, Bernd Jochen Hilberath, and Zwi Werblowsky, *How Can Jews and Christians Speak about God in the Modern Secular World? Symposium November 22–23, 1995 in the Episcopal Education Center of the Diocese of Berlin.* Münster: Lit-Verlag, 1997]

The following project was suggested and supported by the discussion group:

Günter Biemer and Ernst Ludwig Ehrlich, eds., *Lernprozess Christen-Juden.* 4 vols. Düsseldorf and Freiburg: Herder, 1980ff.

[Günter Biemer and Ernst Ludwig Ehrlich, eds., *The Learning Process of Christians and Jews.* 4 vols.]

The discussion group's publications can all be ordered at: Zentralkomitee der deutschen Katholiken, Hochkreuzallee 246, D-53175 Bonn, or by e-mail: presse@zdk.de.

Contributors to this Book

Appendix C

Mary C. Boys, S.N.J.M.
Skinner and McAlpin Professor of Practical Theology, Union Theological Seminary, New York City

Ernst Ludwig Ehrlich
Former Honorary Professor of Modern Jewish History and Literature, University of Bern, Switzerland; European Director of B'nai Brith, Basel

Eugene J. Fisher
Associate Director, Secretariat for Ecumenical and Interreligious Relations, National Conference of Catholic Bishops (USA)

James L. Heft, S.M.
Professor of Faith and Culture and Chancellor of the University of Dayton (Ohio)

Hanspeter Heinz
Professor Emeritus of Pastoral Theology, University of Augsburg; Chairman of the discussion group "Jews and Christians," Zentralkomitee der deutschen Katholiken

Walter Cardinal Kasper
President of the Pontifical Commission for Religious Relations with Judaism, Rome

Karl Cardinal Lehmann
Bishop of the Diocese of Mainz; President of the German Bishops Conference

Alan Mittleman
Professor of Religion at Muhlenberg College, Allentown, Pennsylvania

John T. Pawlikowski, O.S.M.
Professor of Social Ethics at Catholic Theological Union, Chicago; President of the International Council of Christians and Jews

Michael A. Signer
Abrams Professor of Jewish Thought and Culture, Department of Theology, University of Notre Dame, South Bend, Indiana

Martin Stoehr
Professor Emeritus of Systematic Theology (Ecumenical Theology and Jewish-Christian Relations), University of Siegen